TWO YEARS
BEHIND THE MAST

An American Landlubber at
Sea in World War II

TWO YEARS
BEHIND THE MAST

An American Landlubber at Sea in World War II

by
Lieutenant Commander
Harold J. McCormick, USNR (Ret.)

Sunflower University Press®
1531 Yuma (Box 1009), Manhattan, Kansas 66502-4228 USA

© 1991 by Harold J. McCormick

ISBN 0-89745-138-4

Edited by Roger Friedmann

Layout by Lori L. Daniel

Cover painting, "Death of a Liberty Ship," by marine artist
Herb Hewitt, Wakefield, Massachusetts.

Dedication

To Commander Jurgen Oesten
of German U-boat 861 —
A wartime enemy who has
become a good friend.

The SS *William Gaston*, launched in Baltimore, Maryland, 6 September 1942. The life raft which saved 14 men is visible in its chute on the port side forward.

Contents

Harold J. McCormick, 1945.

Preface

Born in 1914 in Fort Wayne, Indiana, and raised in the Midwest during my teens and early twenties, I grew up with the typical young inlander's fascination with the sea. I thought I might "Join the Navy and See the World," but I did not then really have the temperament for life in the Armed Services.

I had youthful fantasies about adventurous travel on tramp steamers, but really had no sea-going qualifications. I even considered trying to sign on as a crewman on a cattle boat to Europe, where the required skills consisted of little more than a certain dexterity with a shovel in the hold.

My favorite authors at that time were the popular adventure storytellers — Richard Henry Dana, Alan Villiers, Joseph Conrad, Herman Melville, Jack London, Richard Halliburton, Richard Harding Davis, Count von Luckner, Lowell Thomas, Admiral Byrd, Nordhoff, Hall, and others.

By the mid-1930s I had completed my formal education (rather inadequately, by the way), had secured a position as a reporter on the Fort Wayne *News-Sentinel*, and later became Manager of Advertising and Public Relations for Indiana Service Corporation, an electric and transit utility. I joined the Fort Wayne Country Club and played a lot of golf. By the late 1930s I began to have visions about "seeing the world" from the decks of cruise ships.

All through the late 1930s, America had watched in growing disgust and contempt the shouting and strutting of Adolph Hitler and Benito Mussolini. When the European war broke out in September 1939, most Americans became supporters of Great Britain and France, despite the fact that our nation's population was far more German and Italian than British and French.

Within a few months President Roosevelt proposed, and Congress enacted, the Selective Service Act of 1940, which called for the registration of all male citizens, their classification by local draft boards, and the calling up of eligible young men for "one year of basic military training in the Army," in a sequence determined by a national lottery.

As I was in good health, unmarried, and not engaged in essential employment, I was almost automatically classified 1A. However, I had the good fortune to draw a relatively high draft number, which gave me time to consider other options.

The Air Force, Navy, Coast Guard, and Merchant Marine had attractive programs to attract volunteers, but all of these involved commitments longer than one year.

One of my golfing partners, Jack Mueller, had a low draft number and was called up early. When he returned home on leave he gave us a depressing report on military life, saying the Army had two basic operating practices — "No. 1: Hurry, No. 2: Wait."

When the Japanese attacked Pearl Harbor and America was drawn into the war in December 1941, the concept of "one year of basic training" became an anachronism. Everyone would be "in for the duration." I decided at once to join the Navy.

What follows is the true story of how one 27-year-old Midwesterner fulfilled his military duty as a citizen and also realized his boyhood dreams of seeing "faraway places with strange-sounding names." As the title suggests, this book has been inspired by that great nineteenth century American maritime classic *Two Years Before The Mast* (*i.e.*, in the crew forecastle), by Richard Henry Dana, which I first read some 60 years ago. Although I would not presume to equate my own modest book with that great classic, both describe the experience of young landlubbers in their first two years at sea.

Because of twentieth century technology, it was possible for me to sail greater distances and to visit more remote places than Dana could only dream of seeing; and, because of World War II, I witnessed modern machine-versus-man mayhem, which even he could hardly have imagined 150 years ago.

In addition to my own personal recollections, many of the names, places, and dates cited in this book have been secured from declassified wartime U.S. Navy documents obtained from the Naval Historical Center and the National Archives in Washington, D.C. — for which I thank all concerned.

HJM 1990

Foreword

Hal McCormick and his lovely wife, Helen, sure know how to throw a party. When I was in his home in Stamford a few years back, he had in the room a sailing ship restorer, an Australian merchant seaman, myself who works for an historical society, the distinguished marine artist Herb Hewitt (whose painting of Hal's ship the *William Gaston* adorns the front of this book), and Commander Jurgen Oesten, the man who sank the *William Gaston* 40-odd years earlier, leaving Hal to flounder around on a life raft in the windy reaches of the South Atlantic.

Stirred by his wide-ranging curiosity, his desire to get out there and find out about things that characterize the man, he had found out the identity of the *U-boat 861* that sent the Liberty ship *William Gaston* to the bottom with a couple of well-placed torpedoes on the night of 23 July 1944. Many years later, he learned the skipper's name, hunted him down in Germany, became a friend to him, and capped this effort by holding a reception for him in his Connecticut home. A thorough-going, decent, and seamanly thing to do — again, characteristic of the man.

Hal was raised in Fort Wayne, Indiana. He had no particular reason to turn to the sea, except that general desire to get out in the world, meet its varied denizens, and find out what makes it tick. World War II gave a swift boost to this desire, propelling Hal to remote and unlikely corners of the ocean world in command of the U.S. Naval Armed Guard which was put aboard ships to man the guns with which a Merchant ship was supposed to defend herself against attack by hostile aircraft and submarines, or, more rarely, surface warships.

Hal's ship was far from alone in succumbing to submarine attack. Of some 2,710 Merchant ships of the *Gaston's* class, built as an emergency measure to supply the battle fronts of a worldwide conflict, over 200 failed to come home. Wartime service in these ships was more dangerous, as it turned out, than service in warships, in the Air Corps, or ashore with the Army.

Hal is very aware of the war that convulsed the world during his voyaging. He reports the news from the battle fronts as it reached the men at sea and ashore, recalling tense and anxious days. At one point, this crazy young fellow hitchhikes to the battlefront in Italy, just to look up a friend! Friendship, one of the most precious things in the world then or now, is a lot of what Hal's book is about.

And of course the book is good history — good because it's so real, recalled in such total detail in the vivid colors of real-life events, by a person with a knack for making adventures happen.

It isn't the dangers of his time at sea that you'll find yourself thinking of as you dip into Hal's account of his wide-ranging, event-filled wartime years at sea, rather it's the friends he makes, the conversations he gets into — whether in the Henry Hudson Hotel on Manhattan's West 58th Street, or the cabaret Ta-Ba-Ris in Buenos Aires, or in the night watches on the bridge of a freighter chugging along — and the very Catholic sense that all this matters, that a compellingly real picture is coming into being under your eyes.

As I said, Hal throws quite a party. I'm very glad to have been invited to this one.

Peter Stanford
President
National Maritime Historical Society
Croton-on-Hudson, NY 10520

Chapter 1

1942 —
Great Lakes, Illinois

In early January 1942, after spending the Christmas and New Year's holidays with my family in Fort Wayne, I drove to Great Lakes Naval Training Station in my 1938 Plymouth Coupe to enlist in the Naval Reserve. Passing through Chicago, I stopped for a luncheon date with a girlfriend. I still remember the charming little French restaurant, La Petite Gourmet, on North Michigan Avenue. Later I visited a flower shop in the neighborhood, managed by a French lady, who was an ally in my courtship.

At Great Lakes, at that time, the Navy was recruiting administrative personnel as well as future sea-going sailors. I enlisted as a yeoman and was assigned, without even attending boot camp, to the Ninth Naval District Security Office (DSO), Captain Felix McWhirter, USNR, of Indianapolis. That office was responsible for antisabotage protection of Naval and Coast Guard facilities and their defense contractors in the Ninth District, which embraced 14 Midwestern states.

I spent the first day completing forms, being interviewed, and undergoing the usual physical examinations. During the latter process, I noted a considerable number of Navy seamen with X's painted on their chests. These, I learned, were volunteers for U.S. submarines, who were given extra physiological and psychological testing to determine their fitness for the rigors of submarine service.

I'll never forget my first night in a Navy barracks. For anyone who has ever entered a military service, it must be the loneliest night of one's life — a strange kind of imprisonment, a world separated from home, family, and friends, with an uncertain future largely beyond one's control. However, I soon became acquainted with other men under the same circumstances and established friendships, which alone make military life bearable for most men.

My first night in the barracks also brought a minor development, which was to have a major impact on my life in the coming months. The public address system carried the very reasonable, but to me very distressing announcement, that effective immediately the Bureau of Naval Personnel (BuPers) had ordered that all Navy officers and enlisted men were to wear their uniforms at all times, whether on or off duty. With that announcement came the end of all civilian lifestyle and the beginning of full-time military duty.

To explain the personal significance of that to me, it is necessary to recall certain events in my life between 1940 and 1941. During those years I had been making modest progress in my business career, living a bachelor's life, and playing golf regularly at the Fort Wayne Country Club.

There was one particularly glamorous young lady — a Sigourney Weaver look-alike — who dated a number of the young unmarried male members with varying degrees of eligibility, including myself.

I was always aware that she was more attracted to Ken Ryan, one of my close friends and golfing partners, than she was to me. However, in that crazy brink-of-war world, Ken had the misfortune to draw a lower draft number than mine. As a result, when he was called for basic training in the U.S. Army, I was able to date her regularly until late 1941, when she moved to Chicago to work in interior decorating. I drove her to Chicago in her Packard Convertible Touring Car and then took the train back to Fort Wayne.

One day that fall, I happened to see in a local gift shop window a cute Hummel porcelain figurine depicting a young girl on skis who had fallen on her backside in the snow, with her legs and skis in the air.

It reminded me of my girlfriend, who had taken up skiing before it was really fashionable in Indiana. She was then working at a shop called Moderne Interiors in Chicago and was living at a private hostelry, The Three Arts Club.

I bought the firgurine and sent it to her, along with a bit of doggerel verse which I still remember:

> Up in "Chi" lives a gal quite superior,
> Knows Three Arts and the Moderne Interior.
>   So artistic is she
>   That when out to ski
> She blackens and blues her posterior.

She came home for the Christmas holidays, and we went to several "open-house" parties together. We also attended midnight mass on Christmas Eve, which I remember because it was then that I learned for the first time that she had a lovely singing voice.

Main Gate

U. S. NAVAL TRAINING STATION, GREAT LAKES, ILLINOIS
REAR ADMIRAL, JOHN DOWNES U. S. NAVY, COMMANDING OFFICER

Two 1942 views of the U.S. Naval Training Station, Great Lakes, Illinois. Above: The Main Gate on Sheridan Road. Below: The Administration Building for the Ninth Naval District Headquarters. The District Security Office was located on the second floor, left end of the building. Lake Michigan is unseen in the background. (Photos, U.S. Navy, courtesy of Naval Historical Center, Washington, D.C.)

At that time, all single men in good health were considering their own options for inevitable military service. I was always more interested in the Navy than the Army, Air Force, or Marines. However, I had always had a kind of mental block about the uniforms of Naval enlisted men. I felt then, and still feel, that Army, Air Force, and Marine uniforms were and are relatively democratic — officers' and enlisted men's varying mostly by insignia. By contrast, the Navy uniforms for enlisted men were based on eighteenth century British designs and seemed to be a planned part of the Navy's discipline system. There was the rationale, of course, that enlisted men's uniforms could be "rolled" and packed in sea bags.

For a man who had spent nearly ten years in business suits, it was a rather traumatic experience to change to the Navy's "dress blues" of bell-bottomed trousers, middy blouses with sailor collars, and so-called "flat" hats. The "summer whites" seemed even more demeaning.

When I enlisted in the Navy at Great Lakes, I was in my chosen service and hoped eventually "to go to sea and see the world." However, I also had the selfish idea that for a time at least I could see my girlfriend in Chicago while wearing civilian clothes. The BuPers announcement ended that pipe dream.

I knew that my friend was socializing with commissioned officers from nearby military bases and candidates from officer-training schools. I felt I would be out of place in such an environment, and I didn't try to see the girl for over a year, although I periodically sent her greeting cards, notes, and flowers.

However, my Naval duties at Great Lakes were proving very rewarding. My first assignment was one of the most challenging of my life. Captain McWhirter, still organizing his new command, handed me a file and said, "See what this is all about, and what we should do about it." It was a fairly recent directive from the Bureau of Naval Personnel to Commandants of all Naval Districts, ordering the establishment of a new identification card system for all Naval and Coast Guard personnel. Ultimately, it involved an enormous mass of administrative details — recruiting photographer's mates, acquiring high-priority equipment and supplies like identification cameras and film, darkroom development facilities established in an old brig, van trucks as mobile identification units, and the photographing, serial-numbering, and thumb-printing of 50,000 Navy and Coast Guard personnel at different intervals while they were being transferred throughout a 14-state district. To this very day, I am still appalled to think of the complexity of that project.

Throughout the spring of 1942, due to a shortage of officers, I, as a yeoman, was the Petty Officer-in-Charge of the Identification Section. In that capacity, I drafted a number of directives for the signatures of Captain McWhirter and Rear Admiral John Downes, Commandant of the Ninth Naval District. On one occasion, I submitted a draft to Lieutenant Samuel R. Sutphin, USNR, of Indianapolis, who was Chief-of-Staff to Captain McWhirter. The directive said something like "The Admiral is anxious that, etc." I'll never forget Sutphin's admonition to me: "Harold, admirals are never *anxious* about anything. . . ."

In early summer, the following newly commissioned Reserve Officers were assigned to the operation: Lieutenant (jg) Nelson Deranian, of Indianapolis; Ensign Norfleet H. Rand, of St. Louis, and an attractive red-headed WAVE Ensign from Salt Lake City, whose nickname was "Rusty" but whose surname regrettably I am unable to recall. These were really favorable developments for our project as they enhanced our ability to deal with the various departments and commands in the Ninth District whose cooperation was essential to our success.

Other new officers and civilian employees joining the DSO staff were Ensign Robert Orr and Special Agent Judd Leighton, both of South Bend, Indiana. Bob Orr was somewhat overage for his rank and joked that he was "the Navy's Bull Ensign."

At Great Lakes Naval Station in 1942 — as at *all* military establishments *traditionally* — enlisted men were ingenious in their ability to work out ways to "beat the system." A friend of mine, Photographer's Mate Jim Worden, of South Bend, discovered that while it was sometimes difficult to secure a "liberty pass" for an evening off the base, it was always easy to obtain a "property pass" to take a package into town. Therefore, Jim would regularly "dummy up" a phony package, use a property pass as a diversion with the Marine Guard at the Main Gate, and "go ashore" whenever he ostensibly wanted to remove property, even though he had no permission to leave the station himself!

* * *

Although America's war had started in the Pacific, it first struck home in the Atlantic when, after the Axis Powers had declared war on the United States, German U-boats began operating off the East Coast in January 1942. The U-boats were aided at night by the bright lights of seacoast cities, which silhouetted coastal shipping and provided easy targets for torpedoes. Merchants in resorts like Atlantic City and Miami Beach were reluctant to "black out" because of the adverse effect on tourist business. But they got the message when oil from sunken tankers began washing up on the beaches.

The U.S. Navy could not provide enough convoy protection — because of a shortage of escort vessels — and resorted to appeals to private pleasure-craft owners to lend their boats to the Navy for offshore patrols.

One of my friends, Jack Morris, had an interesting experience in connection with all this. He had been commissioned an ensign in the U.S. Coast Guard, and his first assignment was to take command of a small private yacht stationed at Norfolk, Virginia. On his *first night* at sea he was awakened by a bright light shining through the portholes. Running up on deck, he saw a U-boat on the surface a short distance off. Then, in crisp English, a voice shouted through a megaphone, "You should stop annoying us with your flea-boats. I will give you two minutes to abandon ship before I sink it." Inasmuch as Jack's "armament" was limited to one .30-caliber machine-gun, he took the advice, abandoned ship, and watched the U-boat sink the yacht with gunfire. On his *first morning* at sea, Jack and his crew were floating in a small dinghy a few miles off Hampton Roads.

Meanwhile, throughout 1942, all of us at Great Lakes, as well as all other Americans, were reading newspapers and listening to radio reports about developments in the war. German and Italian forces (and "neutral" Spain) were fully in control of Continental Europe, and the Japanese were continuing to take over Southeast Asia and the Pacific Islands. German U-boats were having a "turkey shoot" of U.S. Merchant vessels off our East Coast. Among other items of bad news, I remember well the destruction by fire — thought to be sabotage at the time — of the French Liner *Normandie* at a Hudson River Pier in the Port of New York.

However, in May the U.S. Navy scored a brilliant victory over the Japanese in the Battle of Midway, and in November U.S. forces made successful landings at Casablanca and Guadalcanal.

In December I was fortunate enough to obtain a brief leave to spend another Christmas with my family in Fort Wayne — traveling, of course, by trains, which during the war were like USO Clubs on wheels.

Chapter 2

1943 —
Assigned to Armed Guard

Early in 1943, after a year on duty in the District Security Office, Captain McWhirter recommended me to the Bureau of Naval Personnel for a commission as an Ensign, USNR, even though I lacked a college degree, which was qualification number one at that time. The recommendation was endorsed on behalf of Admiral Downes by his Chief-of-Staff, a Captain Carr, USN.

In the spring, almost surprisingly, my appointment came through, and literally overnight, my circumstances and lifestyle changed rather dramatically. One Friday evening, I left the office in bell-bottom trousers, checked out of the barracks, picked up my new uniforms, and on Monday morning reported back to my same assignment in officers' dress blues with one shiny gold stripe — a sort of "three-day wonder."

It happened that several of the bachelor officers in DSO had rented what was called "the Big Log House" in Highland Park, Illinois, on a bluff overlooking Lake Michigan, which was the summer home of a wealthy Chicago family. It was called "the Big House" because there was also "the Little Log House" on the same property.

Among others in that "fraternity" were Lieutenant Sutphin, Lieutenant (jg) Deranian, Ensign Rand, Agent Judd Leighton, and several others. It was what any sailor would have called "great duty." We had a live-in couple as servants, who maintained the grounds, kept house, and prepared meals. We had privately owned cars to commute back and forth to Great Lakes. We had the privileges of a Navy Officers' Club, commissary, and wine mess, and also had daily contact with dozens of attractive WAVE officers and Navy nurses. At cocktail parties we entertained interesting people then on the Great Lakes

Captain Felix M. McWhirter, USNR, an Indianapolis, Indiana, bank president in civilian life, was the author's commanding officer at Great Lakes and was responsible for his promotion from Yeoman to Ensign, USNR. A veteran of both World Wars, Captain McWhirter died in 1983 at the age of 97. (Photo courtesy of his son, Commander Felix T. McWhirter, USNR (Ret.), whom the author met at Great Lakes in 1943 but did not know until 1990 that he was also assigned to Armed Guard.)

scene, including Lieutenant and Mrs. Henry Ford II.

Because I had served as an enlisted man there for over a year, I had picked up a few "street smarts" about the Naval Station. I knew, for example, that the

Training Department had 16 mm film projectors and screens and a library of Navy training films, which could be borrowed for group showings. Therefore, whenever we had a dinner party for our WAVE and nurse friends, I began to provide "movies" for after-dinner entertainment.

The Navy training films were not exactly box office attractions of course. However, our audiences consisted of civilian types who were still trying to remember that a floor was a "deck," a wall a "bulkhead," and a stairway a "ladder," and were still using such clumsy expressions as "the so-called topside." Therefore, it was not too far-fetched that they would watch such Navy classics as *Rules of the Road*, *Piloting*, and *An Introduction to Celestial Navigation*.

One weekend I discovered what I thought was a real winner. The Training Department had a new release with the tantalizing title, *The Hidden Enemy* — certainly a spy story, I assumed. After dinner that Saturday evening, while six or eight couples lined up their chairs theaterwise, I darkened the room and turned on the projector.

I still remember the opening title and its background of military music:

The Bureau of Naval Personnel
U.S. Navy Department
Presents
THE HIDDEN ENEMY

Terrific!

The film featured several Hollywood character actors and actresses. However, it soon became clear that *the hidden enemy* was *not* an Axis spy or saboteur. It was SYPHILIS! For an agonizing number of minutes, our mixed audience was treated to a series of closeups of skin lesions on private parts. The viewers reacted with muffled shrieks and guffaws.

Finally, Lieutenant Sutphin mercifully ended the show by jerking the projector power cord from the wall outlet, but not before the audience was shown how to fit a condom onto the end of a broom handle.

That was the end of our "film festival," although the dinner parties continued.

However, there was a "down side" to all this, too. We began to exchange wry jokes about telling our grandchildren that we had "fought World War II at Great Lakes, Illinois."

One incident was particularly disconcerting. Lieutenant Deranian injured his knee and had to be taken by ambulance to the Great Lakes Naval Hospital, which, at that time, was being filled up with U.S. Marine Corps casualties from Guadalcanal. Several times Deranian was asked by Marines, "How did you get yours, Lieutenant?" And he had to reply, "Playing touch football in Highland Park, Illinois."

* * *

During the summer of 1943, with the war turning more favorably for the Allies, and with patriotic fervor sweeping the country, all of the officers in the DSO made their own decisions regarding wartime duty, most writing the standard form letter to BuPers: "Subject: Sea Duty, Request For."

Captain McWhirter was named Commandant of one of the Pacific Islands recaptured from the Japanese. Sutphin and Rand, after further training, were assigned to Fleet ships in the Pacific. Deranian, who was an Armenian-American and could speak a little Turkish, was recruited by General William "Wild Bill" Donovan's OSS and was later parachuted into Yugoslavia. Agent Leighton, who had all the qualifications for a commission, unfortunately couldn't pass the eye examination and had to remain at Great Lakes.

In my own case, if I had had any "small boat experience," I probably would have been assigned to Amphibious Forces. But, lacking that, I was assigned to Armed Guard, meaning Navy gun crews on U.S. Merchant ships, which was then the "bottom-of-the-totem pole" in the U.S. Naval establishment.

Early in October 1943, after a train trip on the Panama Limited, I reported to the Naval Officers Armed Guard School at Gulfport, Mississippi. Our training was primarily in the firing of Oerlikon 20-mm anti-aircraft machine-guns, 3.5-inch and 5.38-inch dual-purpose guns, at both water-borne and air-borne targets. This was rather "heady stuff" for me, as I had previously never fired anything more powerful than a BB gun.

We also underwent gunnery exercises on a Navy training ship on the Gulf of Mexico. There our biggest gun was an old 5-inch Naval cannon whose explosive charge consisted of gunpowder in cloth bags, which were loaded manually into the breech. After each round was fired and the breech was opened by hand, there was a constant danger that flaming fabric might ignite the next charge. I remembered that over 45 years later when I learned of the tragic accident in a gun turret on the Battleship *Iowa* in April 1989.

My first visits to New Orleans were a great thrill for this rather provincial Hoosier. I visited all the jazz joints and famous restaurants in the French Quarter. I acquired a lifelong taste for shrimp prepared in a variety of ways — despite the fact that when I went deep-sea fishing several times on Gulf commercial boats, we were provided with stinking stale shrimp for use as bait.

One evening in a bar on Bourbon Street, I had a chance meeting with an old friend and golfing partner from Fort Wayne — Army Lieutenant Tony Bruggeman. We had several drinks together, brought each other up-to-date on our current situations in the Armed Forces, and parted with mutual exchanges of good luck — and have never met again to this day.

In early December our class was assigned to the Armed Guard Center at New Orleans, one of three serving U.S. coasts. New Orleans was generally considered a preferred location as the Merchant ships usually operated between Gulf ports and Central and South America. The weather was generally mild, and U-boat activity in the Gulf had been intermittent. However, in mid-December, we were told that Armed Guard officers were needed at both San Francisco and Brooklyn, and that all who volunteered could have Christmas leave at home. That did it for me. I volunteered for Brooklyn and left by train for Fort Wayne, looking forward to Christmas at home, but with some trepidation due to reports we had heard about winter crossings on the North Atlantic and especially about the horrors of the Murmansk run to northern Russia.

After spending a reasonably merry Christmas in Fort Wayne, I reported to the Armed Guard Center in Brooklyn, at the end of December — in time to spend my first *and only* New Year's Eve in Times Square.

The Armed Guard Center in Brooklyn deserves some detailed description because it *was* one of the most extraordinary military facilities ever established. It was located in a huge, cavernous old Naval Armory on the East River at the foot of Brooklyn's 52nd Street. At its peak operation, it was headquarters for over 50,000 enlisted men and 2,000 officers. In the Army that manpower would have been divided into four or five divisions with an equal number of general officers. Yet, the Brooklyn Armed Guard Center was directed by a middle-grade officer, Commander William J. Coakley, USN, who had been an enlisted man in World War I and had been commissioned as an officer — what the Navy called "a mustang."

The Brooklyn Center could have been an administrative nightmare, but Commander Coakley and his staff did a remarkable job of organization. Every day hundreds of men, sometimes a thousand or more, would pass in or out of the Center — reporting for duty, being assigned to ships, returning from sea duty, going on or returning from leave, going to or returning from Naval hospitals, or going to or returning from other training or other duty.

The key to the system was a "checklist" customized for every category and status of personnel, directing them where to go and what to do — check in at all pertinent departments — Medical, Dental, Paymaster, Transportation, Training, Ship's Stores, Chaplain, Library, Red Cross, etc. There was never any conversation between Duty Officers and reporting personnel, simply proper identification and the issuance of appropriate checklists. Hundreds of men walked the halls constantly getting checklists initialed. Meanwhile, in the vast center hall, gun crews were being organized or disbanded, others were drilling or exercising, and some were practicing signals by flag or blinker lights. Mess for enlisted men operated 24 hours a day. It was all highly

Exterior and interior views of the Brooklyn Armed Guard Center at 52nd Street and the East River. The old Naval Armory was razed during the 1950s. The main deck of the interior served 24 hours daily as mess hall, movie theater, bandstand, drill hall, etc.

Above: The AG Center outside drill area with 20-mm anti-aircraft guns and 5.38-inch dual-purpose gun for training. (Photo, U.S. Navy, courtesy of National Archives)

Below: Commander Andrew J. Coakley, USN, in charge of the Brooklyn AG Center, was the author's commanding officer for two years, though the two men never met. (Photo, U.S. Navy, by Navy Photographer's Mate Clarence F. Korker)

organized, but to a visitor it would have looked like a scene from *Hellz apoppin* or *You Can't Take It With You* — popular Broadway shows of the period.

The officers at the Brooklyn Center were billeted at the Henry Hudson Hotel on West 58th Street in Manhattan, involving a long subway trip every morning and night. Yet, the Henry Hudson was a fun place to live under those circumstances. With the hotel filled with military personnel, every night was Saturday night, and every Saturday night was New Year's Eve, as we never knew when we would be assigned to ships and miss the next party.

In late 1943, New York City, as the main Port of Embarkation for the European theater, was an exciting and vibrant place. There were hundreds of men and women in military uniforms on the streets and in public places, and they were welcome everywhere. The streets were clean and safe as was the subway system, and the five-cent fare was the best bargain in the country.

On a number of occasions I had the experience of walking into a bar and ordering a drink and having another patron say to the bartender, "Joe, put the lieutenant's drink on my tab."

On one memorable evening I had the pleasure, through the good offices of Personnel at the Armed Guard Center, of being one of a dozen bachelor officers to accept the invitation of a prominent New York society matron to join an equal number of young debutantes for a dinner dance at her Park Avenue mansion. We sat at a long table in the ballroom, with an orchestra providing dance music. I believe that was the night I decided I wanted to live in New York City.

Another evening I was one of a few officers who were guests of the Lamb's Club, a New York actors' society, at one of their "roasts." I don't recall who the "roastee" was, but one of the "roasters" was Leo Durocher, manager of the old Brooklyn Dodgers. At that time, I must have been more interested in baseball than the theater.

On another occasion, Lieutenant (jg) Ed Reilly, who had worked for College Inn Foods in Chicago, persuaded several of us at the Henry Hudson to go out for what he promised would be a unique meal. We took the subway down to Greenwich Village, went to an Italian Restaurant, and ate something called *pizza*, which seemed very exotic at that time.

* * *

Early in the war there had been many reports of ill will between Merchant and Navy crews on U.S. ships. Merchant Masters and Armed Guard Officers sometimes distrusted each other and were authorized to report *each other's* deficiencies. Many inexperienced merchant seamen, oilers, wipers, and mess attendants had joined the Merchant Marine because they were subject to military draft. Their wages were far higher than Navy pay, and they also earned bonuses for time spent in designated war zones, which irritated the Navy men. On the other hand, Navy personnel often received hospitality and courtesies ashore, which were not extended to Merchant personnel, thus alienating them. These conditions did not change during the war, but understanding and acceptance of them gradually improved. On the three ships in which I eventually served, relations between Merchant and Navy crews were generally very good.

One memorable experience of every Armed Guard Officer reporting to the Brooklyn Center was Commander Coakley's orientation lecture. I attended one in December 1943 — I think the only time I ever saw the man. He was obviously smart, dedicated, and tough. He described our opportunities, responsibilities, and obligations, and concluded with a statement I remember word for word:

> And now, gentlemen, I have one other subject to cover with you. . . . We have had several instances of Armed Guard Officers seeking to exploit young members of their crew sexually. . . . If any of you have any such inclinations, I strongly recommend that, at the earliest opportunity, you take your service revolver and blow your brains out . . . so we don't have to do it later. Good luck. . . .

One of the Liberty ships converted to an auxiliary troopship, similar to the *William Gaston*, carried U.S. Army Air Forces crews and military cargo to the European theater. (Photo, U.S. Navy, courtesy of National Archives)

Chapter 3

1944 —
Aboard SS *Alfred Moore*

After approximately two weeks at the Brooklyn Armed Guard Center awaiting assignment, on 11 January 1944, I was given orders to report to SS *Alfred Moore*, a U.S. Liberty ship then at anchor in New York harbor, to serve as Junior Armed Guard Commander. I completed my first "Officer Assigned to Ship Check-List," and was provided Navy transportation to the ship along with nine additional Navy personnel.

Alfred Moore was one of the early Liberty ships having been launched at Wilmington, North Carolina, in early 1942. Unlike most Liberties, which were basically freighters, *Alfred Moore* had been outfitted as a troopship, with three of the five holds (#2, #3, and #4) provided with tiers of bunks for military personnel, and holds #1 and #5 reserved for military cargo.

Alfred Moore was owned by the War Shipping Administration, was operated by Prudential Steamship Company of New York, and was under charter to the U.S. Army for the purpose of transporting military personnel to the European theater. The Merchant Master was Captain John J. O'Connor of New York City; the Armed Guard Commander was Ensign John F. O'Donnell, USNR, of Philadelphia. Two Armed Guard Officers and one Communications Officer were assigned because the ship carried troops.

Liberty ships were named in honor of American men and women who had been well-known public figures in the eighteenth and nineteenth centuries. Alfred Moore was born in North Carolina in 1755, served with Colonial forces in the Revolutionary War, later became a lawyer and state attorney general, and was appointed an Associate Justice of the U.S. Supreme Court by President John Adams. He died in 1810.

The Merchant Marine Radio Operator was Nicholas B. Wynnick of Ansonia, Connecticut, with whom I became only casually acquainted. I had not yet learned that the Radio Operator was really a man to know on Merchant ships as it was possible to visit him in the "radio shack" and listen to both military and civilian broadcasts. We did not become really acquainted until 45 years after the war, when in 1989 he obtained my name and address through the Armed Guard Veterans Association and visited me at our home in Stamford, Connecticut.

Another character aboard *Alfred Moore* worthy of mention was Army Lieutenant Ted Nichpor, of Toledo, Ohio, assigned to the Army Transport Service, which was responsible for billeting and feeding Army troops in transport. Ted told us one of the more amusing stories about Army life which we had heard up to that time.

Ted said that before attending Officer Candidate School, he had been an enlisted man at a camp which was training recruits for service with the Infantry, which was not the preferred duty for most GIs. Ted had a hunch he could avoid being "shipped out" if he could secure an appointment to the camp organization.

Ted had noted that the base military band had no glockenspiel, so he called on the camp bandmaster and told of his playing that instrument in his high school band — which was pure fiction. The bandmaster said he had no glockenspiel, but might be able to requisition one, and arranged for Ted's assignment to the camp band!

Like other Liberty ships, *Alfred Moore* was 7,177 gross tons, 442 feet in length, and 59 feet in beam. Liberties were the first sea-going ships ever built by mass production. Separate sections were fabricated in different factories and were assembled at shipyards by welding rather than riveting. A prime contractor was Kaiser Shipbuilding Company, precursor of automobiles of Kaiser-Frazer fame. Between 1941 and 1945, approximately 2,710 Liberty ships were built; and although there was concern about their breaking up in heavy seas (a few did), they represented a major American contribution to the war in all theaters around the world.

The Liberties were powered by oil-fired reciprocating steam engines, which turned one propeller on the stern. They were slow — 8 to 11 knots — but could be built quickly. The newer, faster steam turbine engines turning twin screws were reserved for later classes of vessels like the C-2 cargo ships and T-2 tankers.

The Liberty's midship house consisted of four levels. The first, on the main deck, was nearly as wide as the ship itself, except for narrow outside passageways along each rail. This level housed the crew quarters, both Merchant and Navy, plus the galley and two mess halls, one for officers and one for crew, each serving the same food. On the inside passageways, both port and starboard, there were doors leading below to the engine room, which was reached by steel ladders and catwalks.

The second level was the boat deck, which housed individual staterooms for the ship's officers and Navy Armed Guard Commander. The enclosed area was much smaller than the first level because of the open-air deck provided for lifeboats.

The third level was the bridge deck, which housed the Captain's stateroom, the "radio shack," the wheel house with the engine room telegraph, and a separate room with files of navigation charts, a charting desk, and a gyrocompass. There were also doors opening onto the wings of the bridge on the port and starboard sides.

On top of the Captain's deck was the flying bridge, an open-air deck for 360° visibility, with separate controls for the ship, plus four steel tubs equipped with 20-mm anti-aircraft guns. The flying bridge was also the communications center for the Navy gun crew, with sound-powered (non-electric) telephone lines to the bow and stern gun platforms.

For lifesaving equipment, in addition to life jackets and life rings, the Liberties were provided with four lifeboats, located on the boat deck, and four life rafts mounted in slide racks on the main deck, fore and aft of the midship house. On *Alfred Moore* there also were portable life rafts for Army personnel.

On *Alfred Moore* the defensive armament consisted of eight 20-mm Oelirkon anti-aircraft guns, one 3.5-inch anti-aircraft/anti-ship gun on the bow, and one 4-inch anti-ship gun on the stern. The main guns were rarely used in action, but served an important purpose in helping to keep U-boats submerged during daylight. This was a major consideration because U-boats were relatively slow when submerged but very fast on the surface.

I will never forget that day in January 1944 when I first boarded *Alfred Moore* in New York Harbor. First of all, the weather was bitterly cold and windy, there was floating ice in the harbor, and the stateroom I was to share with the Communications Officer, had been newly constructed on the Captain's deck and was exposed to the weather on three sides. Keeping warm was impossible; keeping from freezing was an achievement in itself. Fortunately, the Communications Officer turned out to be Ensign Robert D. Barnard, USNR, of Indianapolis, with whom I shared a number of Hoosier friends.

* * *

On 13 January 1944, *Alfred Moore* sailed independently from New York for Norfolk, Virginia, arriving there on 14 January. Before entering Hampton Roads, we were delayed in going to the dock, which I recall annoyed Captain O'Connor because of his recollection of U-boat activity in that area in 1942 and 1943.

One evening at the Officer's Club at Norfolk Naval Station, I had a chance meeting with an old friend and golfing partner from Fort Wayne — Navy Lieutenant Al Randall. We had several drinks together, brought each other up to date on our current situations in the Armed Forces, and parted with mutual exchanges of good luck — and have never met again to this day. Does that sound familiar?

After taking aboard about 400 Army Air Forces personnel plus military cargo, *Alfred Moore* sailed from Norfolk on 23 January, but rode at anchor in Hampton Roads pending a convoy conference at Little Creek, Virginia, on 24 January, which was attended by Captain O'Connor, newly promoted Lieutenant (jg) O'Donnell, Ensign Barnard, and myself.

This was the first of many convoy conferences I attended during the war and will always be memorable to me. Present were the Merchant Masters and Gunnery and Communications Officers of all ships, U.S. and Allied. The group was briefed by the Commodore of the Convoy, as usual a Commander or Captain of the regular U.S. Navy who was in command from the lead ship, a U.S. or Allied passenger liner being used as a troopship; also by the Escort Commander, a USN officer in a destroyer (DD) or destroyer-escort (DE); and finally, by Naval Intelligence Officers, using charts to illustrate recent U-boat activity on the prospective course. We were told that we would be a "slow convoy" — about eight knots — to Gibraltar and the Mediterranean, but the exact destination of each ship was not revealed.

On 25 January, *Alfred Moore* sailed from Hampton Roads, along with other ships from that port, and during the day joined other ships from other Atlantic Coast ports. By the following morning we were in a convoy consisting of more than 100 ships and 10 to 15 U.S. Navy escort vessels, in 10 single-line columns and rows of 10 or more ships each.

As a troopship, *Alfred Moore* was in a middle column and middle row. Our view was of a vast armada of ships, stretching to the horizon in all directions. The huge Allied Atlantic convoys of World War II were perhaps the largest manmade spectacles in history. A Cecil B. DeMille movie extravaganza was Lilliputian by comparison.

In such a large convoy, communications were a major problem; and in early 1944 these were still pretty primitive. While the Commodore and Escort Commander could communicate by low-power, two-way radio, most Merchant ships had no such capability. Therefore, if the Commodore wished to make a change of course (which was frequently necessary every 24 hours), he had no means of communication to the convoy except Morse code signals by blinker light, first passed to lead ships in each column and then down each column to the last ship. It could take a half hour or longer to signal a 10° change of course.

At other times the Commodore could institute a zigzag plan by signaling the

plan number. At night all ships were ordered to "black out," except for a small
blue light on each ship's lower stern, which enabled following ships to
maintain station by visual observation through binoculars.

Between 25 January and 10 February, the convoy proceeded eastward
toward the Straits of Gibraltar. On 31 January, 1 February, and 10 February, the
Commodore signaled "submarines in vicinity." Escort ships dropped depth
charges, but no U-boats were observed on the surface.

During the crossing there were a number of observations worthy of
mention. There were several Dutch ships in the convoy whose masters had fled
Holland with their wives and family and whose ships sometimes carried
laundry on clotheslines and children playing on the deck. Another chilling
sight would be seen when old Merchant vessels broke down and had to drop
out of the convoy, and the Commodore had to make difficult decisions as to
whether, and for how long, an escort ship could be detached to stand by and try
to protect the stragglers.

During the crossing, the Army mess operated from daylight to dark but still
could serve only two meals in each 24 hours. The Air Forces personnel,
trained to the freedom of the skies, obviously felt a kind of claustrophobia in
confinement below decks of a ship. And well they should have — one torpedo
below the waterline would have made their survival virtually impossible.

One evening, following the usual sunset general-quarters watch, the Merchant and Navy officers conducted an abandon-ship training session for Army
personnel deep in #3 hold. Frankly, I could hardly wait to get back up to
topside again. To this day, 46 years later, I still salute the tens of thousands of
U.S. military personnel for their lonely crossings of the Atlantic and Pacific in
the holds of Liberty ships during World War II.

As we approached Gibraltar, we were aware that the Mediterranean was
then the most active theater of the war. During 1943, the Allies had occupied
all of North Africa; held Malta; occupied the islands of Pantelleria and Sicily;
invaded Italy at Salerno, south of Naples; and, in January 1944, while we were
crossing the Atlantic, had by-passed the German's Italian defense line across
Italy by a dramatic landing to the north at Anzio on the Tyrrhenian Sea.

On 11 February, after switching from U.S. to British escorts, our convoy
passed the Rock of Gibraltar and, as on five other such passages during the
war, some wag on board always said, "You see they've taken the Prudential
sign down for the duration." Between 12 February and 15 February, the
convoy passed near Oran and Algiers, Algeria; Bizerte, Tunisia; and the Island
of Malta. On 16 February, the convoy was split into two sections, one going to
the Eastern Mediterranean, while ours sailed northward to Augusta, Sicily,
where we anchored on 17-18 February, then sailed through the Strait of
Messina to the Bay of Naples, where we dropped anchor on 19 February.

The Bay of Naples is widely recognized as one of the most beautiful bodies of water in the world — a deep blue sea, a semicircular coast of rolling green hills topped by Mount Vesuvius and studded by the idyllic isles of Capri and Ischia. Yet, in February 1944, it was the prime supply port for the then bloodiest fighting of the European theater.

Chapter 4

Italy:
February-March 1944

After *Alfred Moore* had ridden at anchor off Naples for 48 hours, her U.S. Army Air Forces passengers were disembarked and taken ashore by British Army boats on 21 February. Because of bomb damage to port facilities and higher priority cargoes in other ships, we did not tie up at Pier "F" in Naples until 23 February.

Because we were told we would be in the Naples area for several weeks discharging and reloading return cargo, Lieutenant O'Donnell set in-port watch schedules for Navy personnel, which gave us all time to "see the sights" of Naples.

Several of us were able to visit the ruins of Pompeii, and later actually climbed up the side of Mount Vesuvius, as I recall, to within 25 to 50 yards of the smoking open crater. Unfortunately, we were unable to make the trip to the Isle of Capri, because of difficulties in arranging auto and boat transportation.

In fact, we soon learned that in Naples (as in war zones everywhere), local transportation was *everything*. For example, the "in" place to go every night (if possible) was a beautiful estate located in the hills overlooking the bay, known as "The Garden of the Oranges." I'm sure hundreds of U.S. military officers who served in Italy will remember it. Originally the private home of a wealthy Neapolitan businessman, it had been used successively as a Fascist Club, an Italian Officers Club, a German Officers Club, and an Allied Officers Club, and the same personnel — waiters, bartenders, musicians — had served there for all the clientele!

At the Garden one evening, Ensign Barnard and I became acquainted with two U.S. Army Air Forces pilots, who were flying fighter-bombers in ground-support missions from a small airstrip outside Naples. During the evening there was a small German air raid on the city, little more than a nuisance raid. Everyone in the Club took their drinks out to the orange grove and watched the tracer shells from anti-aircraft batteries around the city. Everyone agreed, it was "just like a Fourth of July fireworks display."

When the Club closed, the two U.S. pilots, who had a Jeep, wanted us to see their airstrip, and we drove out along dimmed-out roads. The strip was just that — one makeshift runway, no buildings, aircraft parked for the night under trees.

The pilots then Jeeped us back to the ship and joined us aboard for cold-cut sandwiches, which were always available in the mess halls after midnight. When we parted, the airmen agreed to pick us up and drive to the Garden the following evening.

When the Jeep arrived at the dock at about 6 p.m., there was only a driver aboard. Barnard and I hopped in, and, as we drove off, one of us asked, "Where's your friend?" The driver replied, quite matter-of-factly, "Oh, Joe couldn't make it tonight. He was shot down up north this morning."

One night Ensign Barnard and I became stranded in a blackout, couldn't get back to the ship, and appealed to a U.S. Army post for assistance. We were billeted in La Touristica Hotel, a small but beautiful hostelry, but it had had no heat for a number of years. The twin beds were comfortable enough, but the sheets were wet and clammy. The following morning we walked to the pier and learned that *Alfred Moore* had been shifted to an anchorage north of Naples. We walked along the coast until we could see the ship, about a half mile offshore. We were able to hire an Italian fisherman to row us out, but on the way we had to pass through and over a clearly visible mine field!

* * *

In spite of the fact that Naples had been badly damaged by the war and people were living in near-poverty conditions, the San Carlo Opera was staging performances every day. One afternoon I attended a Puccini opera, which was beautifully produced for a full house. Weeks later, back in New York City, I attended another Puccini opera by the San Carlo Road Company, and, following the performance, went backstage to introduce myself to the Italian cast and tell them that San Carlo was still alive and well in war-torn Naples.

Perhaps my most memorable experience in Italy came about like this. Upon arrival, the *Alfred Moore* crew had received very welcome mail from the States. Among other items, I received a V-mail letter from Sergeant Delbert "Dub" Welch, U.S. Army, who had been a classmate and neighbor of mine in Fort Wayne. Because of censorship, Dub was unable to tell me where he was,

Above: The Bay of Naples, Italy, with Mount Vesuvius in the background and Allied warships at anchor.

Below: The Allied Officers Club in "Garden of the Oranges" in the hills north of Naples. (Photos, U.S. Navy, courtesy of National Archives)

but the general tone of his letter suggested Italy.

The next day, in Naples, I went to the Allied Peninsular Base Command, as I think it was called. I talked to an American Army duty officer and showed him the number of Welch's unit on the envelope. He took me inside into the map room and showed me where the unit was located, just south of Monte Cassino, which was then *the* pivotal point in the entire Italian campaign.

I asked the officer if it would be possible for me to get up there, and he said, "If you're crazy enough to go up there, lots of our guys who *have to* go up there will be glad to give you a lift. Just get out on the main road early in the morning . . . and good luck!"

After clearing my watch duties on the ship, I did decide to go to Welch's unit and was out on the north-bound road early the following morning. And, sure enough, it was easy to hitch a ride in an Army convoy. I rode in a weapons carrier. We stopped at Caeserta for Army mess, and at nightfall I found Welch and his buddies in the basement of an abandoned farmhouse just below Monte Cassino. Along the way I had my first opportunity to observe the results of modern warfare, seeing a number of wrecked tanks, crashed aircraft, and piles of expended artillery shells.

In school, Dub had always excelled in mathematics, and, perhaps surprisingly, the Army had discovered that. He was in charge of a small unit equipped with calculators, preparing ranges and angles for big U.S. guns positioned in an orchard above the farmhouse, shelling German positions around Cassino. The original objective was to try to spare the centuries-old Benedictine monastery atop the mountain, but it was eventually destroyed with the approval of Pope Pius XII.

Welch and his friends and I spent the whole night talking in an abandoned farmhouse which served as their base, periodically interrupted by booming artillery. We shared several Hershey Bars and bottles of Coca Cola, which I had carried in the deep pockets of my insulated Navy parka for possible use as emergency rations. Before leaving the ship that morning I had briefly considered whether I should carry the .45-caliber pistol which the Navy had issued to me. However, I quickly dropped that idea, reasoning that if there was any chance I might need a gun, I shouldn't make the trip.

I was the unit's guest for evening and morning mess served by a mobile Army kitchen, and I was impressed with the abundance and quality of the food — scrambled eggs with sausage for breakfast! However, I was saddened to see Italian farmers and their families, normally producers of food, standing around in the background with buckets and pans to receive leftovers from GI mess kits.

* * *

Following breakfast, I was able to hitch a ride back to Naples in an Army

Jeep and was back aboard ship by evening after an unforgettable 36-hour side trip into the land and air war.

In the middle of one night while we were at anchor north of Naples, the entire crew was awakened by the ringing of a general alarm aboard ship, due to another small German air raid. The Navy crew manned the guns, but we did not fire as we could see no planes in the dark sky. Much later I learned that, on the American recaptured islands in the Pacific, U.S. Marines were often awakened in the middle of the night by a lone Japanese plane overhead. They nicknamed the Jap pilot "Piss-Call Charley."

On or about 1 March, we received another delivery of mail from the States. This time there was a letter from my brother, advising that my father had died in February in Fort Wayne after a short illness, and suggesting that I try to get home at the earliest feasible opportunity.

On 3 March, *Alfred Moore* was ordered to the small port of Bagnoli in the Gulf of Pozzuli to pick up its return cargo — a load of expended brass artillery shells, which were to be returned to the U.S. for refilling or recycling. Due to bad weather, which several times broke the ship's mooring lines, loading was not completed until 8 March, when the ship returned to Naples, joined a new convoy, and headed south toward the Strait of Messina, passing the volcanic isle of Stromboli, which was then in colorful eruption.

Following a 26-day passage in convoy through the Mediterranean and across the Atlantic, *Alfred Moore* arrived in the Port of New York on 4 April, at which time I was relieved by an Ensign Hildeman and was given an emergency 10-day leave because of my father's death — but not, of course, until I had completed an "Officer-Going-on-Leave Check-List."

While visiting with family and friends in Fort Wayne, I phoned my erstwhile girlfriend in Chicago and asked if I might go there and take her to lunch. She accepted, and I was soon on a Pennsy train to the Windy City.

I remember feeling very proud in my new Navy officer's uniform. I had by then been promoted to Lieutenant (jg) and, while most officers wore summer uniforms of cotton khaki, which became shiny and wouldn't hold a press, I had several custom tailored of tan wool gabardine.

Over lunch at a restaurant near my friend's office, I showed her a collection of photographs I had taken surreptitiously on my trip to Italy — ships and escorts in convoy, the bomb-damaged docks in Naples, and wrecked aircraft and tanks I had seen en route to Monte Cassino. Regrettably and stupidly, I later took the prints *and negatives* to sea again and lost them forever.

During lunch I asked her if she would like to see *Oklahoma*, the great Rodgers and Hammerstein musical, which had just opened in Chicago. She assured me that that was impossible as the show was sold-out for weeks ahead.

Nevertheless, after lunch I went to the old Erlinger Theater, where there was a long line of people outside the box office. While awaiting my turn I could overhear discussions about reservations, four, six, or eight weeks in advance. When I reached the window, a rather fatherly looking middle-aged agent said, "And you, Lieutenant, I suppose you need two for tonight. Right? Well, I've got 'em for you."

I always remember that experience as an example of the respect and affection which the American people extended to their men and women in uniform during World War II.

After the show I took the midnight train back to Fort Wayne, and a few days later was off to New York again, feeling much better about my renewed contact with my prewar girlfriend.

For some days afterward I found myself humming the great songs from *Oklahoma*:

> Oh, what a beautiful morning —
> Oh, what a beautiful day,
> I have a wonderful feeling —
> Everything's going my way.

I had no way of knowing at the time, and would not have believed, that our attendance at *Oklahoma* was to be my last date ever with a dear friend.

Chapter 5

1944 —
Aboard SS *William Gaston*

On 5 May 1944, I was assigned as Naval Armed Guard Commander on the U.S. Liberty ship SS *William Gaston*, Merchant Master Harry W. Chase of New York City. The ship then was in the Port of New York, having recently arrived following a voyage from Takoradi, Ghana, West Africa.

Other senior Merchant officers were Chief Mate Ernest Chalk, a former British Master, who had retired to run a pub in Bermuda, and Chief Engineer Gustav Seaberg, a Swedish-American of Yonkers, New York. The ship was owned by the War Shipping Administration and was operated by American-West African Lines of New York.

All Liberty ships were named in honor of deceased American historical personalities, men and women. William Gaston was a prominent New England lawyer, who had served as Mayor of Boston and later as Governor of Massachusetts after the Civil War.

I was assigned a crew of 25 Naval personnel — 4 Petty Officers and 21 Seamen First Class. The facilities and armament were the same as on *Alfred Moore* except that we had a more sophisticated 5.38-inch dual-purpose, surface-and-air gun on the stern.

One day early in May, while our ship was being loaded at Erie Basin in Brooklyn, I took the subway to Manhattan for another day in the big city. On the train I read *The New York Times*, which carried a front-page article about a conference on Pan American postwar trade, then in progress at the Waldorf-Astoria under the auspices of Nelson A. Rockefeller, U.S. Coordinator of Inter-American Affairs.

Inasmuch as we had been alerted that *William Gaston* might be sent to South

America, I felt some interest in the meeting and decided to see if I could crash it.

I went to conference headquarters at the Waldorf and introduced myself to a member of the staff. I explained that our American Liberty ship was sailing for South America, and I wondered if I might be permitted to sit in at one or more of the sessions.

The aide thought about my proposal for a few moments, then excused himself and disappeared into a nearby office. A few minutes later another gentleman came out of the office and said, "Good morning, Lieutenant. I'm Nelson Rockefeller. We're delighted to have a Navy officer interested in this meeting. Please be our guest for lunch."

I accompanied him down to the Cert Room off the main lobby, where I was introduced to a number of the conferees and was treated like a guest rather than a crasher.

At lunch I sat at a round table with about a dozen North and South American business executives. Inasmuch as I had just returned from Italy, which was then the primary theater of the European war, my table companions were very interested in my recent experiences, and during lunch, I felt like the center of attention, not an outsider.

Later, at the first opportunity, I wrote a letter to Mr. Rockefeller to thank him for his hospitality. To my surprise, he responsed and told me he would appreciate receiving my impressions of South America. That began a periodic correspondence which continued for the balance of the war.

* * *

On 15 May, Captain Chase and I attended a convoy conference at the Whitehall Building in lower Manhattan to receive our orders and sailing instructions. On the same day, *The New York Times* carried a three-inch item on an inside page reporting that another Liberty ship, SS *William M. Welch*, had recently broken up and gone down in a storm off Scotland with a loss of 60 lives.

Our orders directed the *William Gaston* to the east coast of South America, but Captain Chase and I were very skeptical. The Allied invasion of Europe was then imminent and we thought our orders might be a "cover story."

On 16 May, *William Gaston* sailed from New York in convoy to Guantanamo, Cuba, and Port of Spain, Trinidad — 40 ships to Cuba and 20 to Trinidad. On the first day out of New York, the escorts dropped depth charges but no results were noted. Otherwise, the voyage was very pleasant in the late spring weather in 20° to 30° North latitude.

On 21 May, during general-quarters watch at sunset, Captain Chase and I were on the flying bridge, surveying the convoy and its escorts through binoculars as we were passing southward through the Bahama Islands. At one point, he called me to the port side and pointed into the distance, saying:

You see that small island in the distance? That's San Salvador. It used to be known as Watling Island. That's the place where Columbus first landed in 1492. It's a beautiful, unspoiled island. Never really been commercialized. My wife and I spent one vacation there, before the war. Loved it. It's really larger than it looks . . . about 13 miles long by 6 miles wide. There are beautiful beaches and cliffs on all sides, and fresh water lakes in the interior. It's almost the same today as when Columbus landed there more than 400 years ago.

And, you know what, I've often thought that Columbus may have found the loveliest spot in the New World at his first stop. He thought it was part of India, and called the natives "Indians." As a result, all of the Europeans who later migrated to the Western Hemisphere perpetuated Columbus' mistake by calling all aborigines "Indians." To this day, even the descendants of all those non-Indian peoples still think of themselves as "Indians." Crazy, isn't it?

As the convoy sailed into the Caribbean en route to Guantanamo, my principal recollection is that the sea was the calmest and smoothest I ever saw before or later. Off Cuba, *William Gaston* left the main convoy and sailed southward with nine other ships.

Arriving in Port of Spain, I was thrilled to be on the only tropical isle I had seen up to that time. In a ship's boat en route to the pier, I was startled to see the body of a large dead alligator floating in the bay. We didn't have many alligators in Indiana.

After setting up Navy watch schedules for our stay in port, I had gone ashore primarily to do some sightseeing. At one of the local bars I met an Ensign and a Lieutenant (jg) from one of our U.S. Navy escort ships, with whom I had a few drinks, dinner of some sort, and a lot of conversation.

After dinner we decided to investigate the nightlife on the island. A taxi driver said he would take us to a private club. It was located in a modest single-family house on the outskirts of town. It proved to be a combination bistro and bordello, operated by several native Black women.

After asking the taxi driver to wait, we entered the house, exchanged greetings with our hostesses, sat down in a small living room, ordered, and were served bottles of beer of uncertain origin.

Then, the women told us about their *other services*. The Lieutenant and I were not interested, but the Ensign decided he would like to "change his luck" and entered an adjacent bedroom with one of the women.

Meanwhile, as the Lieutenant and I ordered another beer, I noticed a

portable hand-wound Victrola and a small stack of records on a side table. I
checked the selections, found a recording of Bing Crosby singing "White
Christmas," placed it on the turntable, cranked the machine, and started it.
Bing sang:

> I'm dreaming of a White Christmas. . .
> Just like the ones I used to know. . . .
> When the tree tops glisten and children listen. . . .
> To hear sleighbells ringing in the snow. . . .
> I'm dreaming of a White. . . .

Suddenly, the bedroom door banged open, and the Ensign stomped into the
living room *au naturel* and shouted, "McCormick, you son of a bitch, you've
ruined Christmas for me forever!"

* * *

On 2 June, *William Gaston* sailed from Port of Spain, heading southward in
a convoy of ten ships and four escorts. Our orders directed us to proceed to
Santos, Brazil, to discharge cargo. We *were* going to South America after all.

On 6 June — the famous D-Day of World War II — we learned by ship's
radio that the long-awaited Allied invasion of Europe had been launched from
England across the Channel into Normandy. As we sailed southward along the
coast of Brazil, it seemed that we were involved in a different war.

The following day, 7 June, stands out clearly in my memory. We crossed the
equator, which is a special event for all neophyte sailors (I still have the
colorful scroll issued to me months later by the Navy); and we crossed the
mouth of the Amazon River, where the blue sea turns to brown as the river
carries billions of particles of clay and sand from the interior of Brazil into the
South Atlantic, a scene which is even more impressive from the air, as I also
saw later in the summer.

During the southward voyage, I wrote several multi-addressed letters to my
family and friends back in Fort Wayne and to my girlfriend in Chicago. Copies
of these and other letters were saved by my brother and returned to me after the
war.

The following are excerpts from one letter, which give an insight into the
mood and conditions aboard *William Gaston*. Because of military censorship,
we were forbidden to reveal our exact locations, but I have now inserted these
parenthetically:

In addition to the North Atlantic convoys, the U.S. Navy also escorted Merchant ships on southbound voyages to Guantanamo, Cuba; Port of Spain, Trinidad; and Rio de Janeiro, Brazil. These were generally smooth passages except for a day or two off Cape Hatteras, NC. (Photo, U.S. Navy, courtesy of National Archives)

— At Sea, 8 June 1944

Dear Folks:

This particular leg of the voyage is a little on the tedious side, but we're all kept in good spirits by the bright prospects for the Summer. It should be wonderful. I have books, maps, etc., and am making all sorts of plans. It'll cost money, but I think it's worth it for this once-in-a-lifetime opportunity. We expect to spend at least 10 days at our next port (Santos, Brazil), a week to 10 days at the next (Montevideo, Uruguay), and at least two or three weeks at our next port or ports (Rosario and Buenos Aires, Argentina) before starting back. My duties should not be very pressing, and I'm hoping to be able to get away for a few short excursions into the hinterlands . . . or the bright spots, as the case may be. For example, the place at which we will spend the first 10 days is (according to my books) "overnight by deluxe train" from one of the real showplaces of the world (Rio de Janeiro). We may stop there anyway, going or coming, but I'm certainly going to see the place, one way or another.

Things have been rolling along pretty smoothly on the ship. I can get along okay with the Captain, and the remainder of the Merchant officers are good fellows, but a pretty heterogeneous lot: The Chief Mate is an old British Master, been sailing for 44 years. The Third Mate is a kid from Wisconsin who won't be 21 until sometime this Summer. The Chief Engineer is a Swedish-born naturalized American, Gustav Seaberg of Yonkers, N.Y., and a very likeable guy. The Captain is ex-U.S. Navy, sailing for something like 40 years. The Radio Operator, sailing 15 years, has made over 30 trips to West Africa alone. Our own Navy crew is a pretty good lot, and I haven't had any serious trouble with any of them yet. Unfortunately, one boy suffered a hernia on the first lap (perhaps I work 'em too hard!), and we had to leave him in a hospital at the last port.

The food has been satisfactory enough thus far. But the Merchant crew complains about it all the time. Frankly, they're the most independent bunch of fatherless sons you've ever seen. They've almost got me convinced that the world owes them a living. Take the food, for example: I think I'm accustomed to eating about as well as any of them, probably better than most. Once in a while we *do* have an unpopular menu . . . choice of lamb or veal, for example. I simply pass it up and eat vegetables and dessert . . . but the crew hollers like hell. Of course, I don't really mind as this probably will improve the chow over the long pull, but the crew insists on making an unpleasant scene over everything.

You see, the whole Merchant organization operates under union arrangements which practically encourages inter-departmental feuds of all kinds . . . a kind of mutual, organized blackmail. For example, the Master can "blacklist" any crew member and prevent him from sailing again. On the other hand, the crew (collectively) can "blacklist" the Master and he can't get another ship.

The Master and the Chief Engineer can "break" the Mates or Engineers, respectively. The Master can "report" the Chief Mate, and vice versa. The Deck, Engineer and Steward Departments have certain definite functions aboard ship, and each has a certain amount of independence of the others; however, each can "report" any or both of the others.

And here are a couple of situations which apply to this ship in particular: The deck force . . . nine seamen, all white . . . take orders from the Bosun, a Negro. Or, take the Steward's Department, which is responsible for meals and quarters: The Steward is a Negro; his department is about half white, half colored . . . except in the galley, where there are three cooks — one white (third cook and baker), one Negro (second cook), and one Chinese (first cook). The latter is quite a character. His name, appropriately enough, is Chow Sung. When the crew complains about the food, he just laughs. And why shouldn't he? He eats rice three times a day every day! And, one further interesting note, six members of the Merchant crew are not even U.S. citizens. And then, on top of all that, just add 26 Navy boys full of pranks from 26 different parts of the country, and stir gently until, well, you have an explosion. Gad, is it any wonder I shudder everytime someone knocks at my door at any hour of the day or night, and I wonder, "Oh, God, what is it this time?"

On 17 June, as we approached Rio de Janeiro, the convoy turned to starboard to enter that port and gave us a final "good luck" signal as we headed independently farther south of Santos. Still the wartime tourist, I found our orders a disappointment. I would have much preferred Rio to Santos.

Sailing independently for the first time was a rather eerie experience for me, especially at night. We realized it was not feasible or economical for Naval authorities to provide an escort for a single Merchant ship carrying a low-priority cargo. Yet we also realized that we were a "slow-moving duck" to any U-boat lurking along our course. We were especially aware of this after nightfall as the blacked-out ship sailed slowly southward, the silence punctuated by the constant groan of the engine and the sound of waves slapping against the hull.

Having lived all of my life in urban areas, I was only vaguely aware of the stellar system, as our view of the stars was limited by city lights and obstructions such as trees and buildings. However, on a darkened ship on a vast ocean at night, stars become awesome. Even the smallest and most distant stars become clearly visible, millions of tiny lights forming a kind of dome over the world, stretching from horizon to horizon in every direction.

In two previous trans-Atlantic crossings I had gradually become familiar with the Northern constellations, particularly the Big Dipper and Polaris, which rides in space directly above the North Pole. After a few nights' observations, even a landlubber can estimate a ship's direction and course in relationship to true North. In fact, the Big Dipper also serves as the hands of a gigantic cosmic clock, and as the earth rotates on its axis between sunset and sunrise, it is even possible to estimate the hour by observing the position of the Big Dipper on the northern horizon.

I also had an opportunity to check out another rather interesting phenomenon. In the Northern Hemisphere, water poured into a wash basin forms a clockwise spiral before flowing down the drain. In the Southern Hemisphere it spirals counter-clockwise. I don't try to understand or explain. It just has something to do with gravity and the rotation of the earth.

When a ship sails independently on a trackless ocean, its safety and success depend upon accurate navigation, an ancient science dating back to the Phoenicians, Carthaginians, and Vikings.

Within sight of land, the method is known as piloting, in which the ship's position is charted continuously by means of direction-finder observations of identifiable points ashore shown on navigation charts. At sea, it is necessary to navigate by the sun or the stars, using sextants to determine the exact angle of their elevation above the horizon at precise points in time. The sun is normally "shot" at midday. The stars can only be "shot" at sunrise or sunset as those are the only times when both horizon and stars are visible. The ship's position is plotted continuously on a navigation chart in order to record progress and be available immediately in case of emergency.

On *William Gaston*, navigation was the responsibility of Chief Mate Chalk, who preferred to take star sights during his regular "4 to 8" watches, rather than sun sights at noon, when he was otherwise free for lunch, reading, sleeping, or supervising his deck crew.

Chapter 6

In Brazil — June 1944

Early on the morning of 19 June, *William Gaston* entered the harbor of Santos, which was and still is the major coffee-exporting port of Brazil. Almost incongruously, as it now seems, there was an enormous billboard-spectacular type of sign advertising "CINZANO" built into a hill on the starboard side of the inward channel. I didn't even know what that product was at the time, but before leaving Santos I had acquired quite a taste for it.

Our stay in Santos — about ten days — was one of the most pleasant interludes of the war for me. The agent for American-West African Lines was an American businessman, James Bacon. He entertained Captain Chase and myself on several occasions at lunch or dinner, and introduced us to a number of his Brazilian friends. I found the Brazilians to be most friendly to *Norte Americanos*, although they were very proud and not reluctant to point to the interior and say, "We have more natural resources than you have" — which, I guess, was true.

However, I experienced one interesting example of Brazilian or South American political mentality. I wanted to visit Sao Paulo, the new city being built from scratch on the piedmont of southern Brazil. I actually made the trip, by funicular railway, and saw wide boulevards and tall buildings suspended in construction because of shortages of critical materials — but *not* until my one-day trip by train had been cleared *in advance* by the police departments of both Santos and Sao Paulo.

While in Sao Paulo, I was able to hire a taxicab to drive me out to the famous Butantan Institute, one of the world's largest snake farms. This was a rather exotic but gruesome enterprise. Large numbers of venomous snakes of various species were kept in ground-level pens and cages. Periodically, livestock was exposed to snakebites, which infected the animals and caused their immune systems to produce antitoxins. These were later extracted, bottled, and exported to places like India, where snakebite was and still is a major public health problem.

In Santos I had an opportunity to do my first South American souvenir shopping. I discovered and purchased several beautiful butterfly trays. These were attractive, handmade serving platters, fashioned of wood with decorative inlays and glass surfaces, under which colorful butterfly wings were arranged in artistic patterns. Brazil was reported to have a greater number and variety of butterflies than any country in the world.

I found in Brazil — and later in other South American countries — that there was not much evidence of a social middle class as we know it in the United States. There seemed to be a relatively small upper class and a very large lower class. It was virtually impossible for a foreigner, especially a serviceman or sailor, to establish any sort of social relationship with an upper-class family. The unmarried daughters were accompanied everywhere by a female chaperone, or duenna. Of course, the language barrier was an added problem.

However, there was a demimonde society of girls and women who worked in stores and offices and supplemented their income by serving as hostesses in evenings at bars and restaurants. It was, of course, a form of prostitution, but seemed rather dignified as the game was always preceded by drinks and food, which were abundant and inexpensive. The proprietors or managers of the establishments seemed to be playing the game, too, and outside there were always friendly taxi drivers waiting to drive couples to a hotel or apartment building, where proper identification was always required.

While in Santos, I met in a restaurant an attractive blond woman in her thirties who claimed to be a member of a White Russian refugee family. This led to the inevitable joke aboard *William Gaston* that "Lieutenant McCormick is now studying Russian."

I remember very clearly that she kept on a small table next to her bed a snapshot of an American Merchant Marine officer who had visited Santos earlier in the war. She was waiting and praying for his return — one of perhaps many World War II versions of Madame Butterfly.

One of my fondest memories of Brazil is of the superiority of the coffee. In Santos, brewing coffee was a real ritual in the sidewalk cafes — recently picked beans, freshly roasted and ground, and brewed in a *non-metallic* vessel. The coffee tasted like a hot liqueur. *By comparison*, most coffee I have drunk since then has tasted like rusty bilge water. Most Americans have no idea how really good, fresh coffee can taste.

Thanks to the Brazilian-Portugese lifestyles of *siesta/mañana*, it required nearly two weeks to unload half of our cargo in Santos, and as a result it was not until 24 June that *William Gaston* sailed southward, again independently, bound for Montevideo, Uruguay.

* * *

During the evening of 3 July, I went to the bridge and joined Officer of the Watch Second Mate James V. Pennino, Captain Chase, and Chief Mate Chalk. We were approaching Montevideo, and everyone seemed keyed up for the arrival.

After leaving Santos, a perceptible tension and nervousness had developed aboard the ship, especially during nighttime hours, as most members of the crew had hardly ever sailed during the war without the protection of a convoy. Although the Allied navies had largely won the Battle of the North Atlantic, Nazi Germany was known still to have a large fleet of operational U-boats, which were then believed to be deployed in the more remote areas of the world, such as the South Atlantic and Indian Ocean.

As on all Merchant and Navy ships, the engineering crew of *William Gaston* was only occasionally seen on the main deck and never in the wheel house or on the bridge. Like subterranean creatures, they were either on watch in the engine room below decks or off watch, sleeping in their quarters.

That night, during the 8 to 12 watch, the man in charge in the engine room was Second Engineer John V. Farrar, who communicated with Second Mate Pennino on the bridge through an ancient piece of equipment known as an engine room telegraph, which exchanged simple directions such as "Full Ahead, Half Ahead, Full Astern, Half Astern, Finished with Engines," etc.

Meanwhile, the deck officers were pacing around the wheel house and wings of the bridge, occasionally scanning the darkening horizons through binoculars, even avoiding conversation as if it might be heard by a distant, lurking U-boat Commander. The Captain and Chief Mate puffed on their cigarettes only in the darkness of the wheel house. The entire ship was blacked out and silent, except for the throb of the engine and the sound of rushing water as the bow plowed through the sea.

Finally, Captain Chase broke the silence.

"You know," he said, "when we sail in convoys, I sometimes resent taking orders from the Commodore and the Escort Commanders. But tonight, well, I'd sleep better if we had a couple of destroyers or DEs out there on our beams."

Everyone agreed.

Although it was mid-winter in the Southern Hemisphere, the temperature was mild, the sea was relatively calm, and a million stars were twinkling overhead. Since leaving New York, the Northern constellations and the Big Dipper had gradually disappeared below the northern horizon, and had been replaced to the south by the Southern constellations and the Southern Cross, which points to the South Pole.

Standing with the others on the port wing of the bridge, Captain Chase continued to philosophize:

> In 40 years of sailing all around the world, I've often thought that it's rather ironical that half the people . . . those living in the Northern Hemisphere . . . have never seen the Southern Cross, and the other half, in the Southern Hemisphere, have never seen the Big Dipper.
>
> People living everywhere experience an orderly succession of seasons — spring, summer, autumn, winter — but for we sailors the seasons are not determined by the calendar but by the latitudes. I've experienced blizzards in July and heat waves in December. It's a fool's life, but I wouldn't change it for the world.

Later during the watch, Captain Chase walked into the chart room, followed by Chief Mate Chalk and myself. Studying the navigational chart under a lamp, the Captain noted that the ship's position was then 10 nautical miles off the coast of Uruguay and about 40 miles north of the mouth of Rio de la Plata, which the ship should reach around midnight.

At about 9:30 p.m., Captain Chase said he was going to turn in, but left orders for the officer of the watch to call him when the lookout sighted the lighthouse at Punta del Este, Uruguay, at the entrance to Rio de la Plata.

Chief Mate Chalk and I continued to stand on the port wing of the bridge. I had become fond of him and an admirer of his since I had joined the ship in New York. He was one of the old school of British Merchant Masters — experienced, competent, dignified, articulate, and soft-spoken. Although he had commanded his own ships for many years, he seemed perfectly happy and willing to serve as Chief Mate on an American ship if that would aid the Allied war effort. He said:

> Even though I have spent my entire career in the English Merchant Marine, I really love the British Navy. I would have preferred serving in the Royal Navy . . . but, as a poor and uneducated sailor from Liverpool, I could never have become an officer in the Navy. I've been better off where I am.

Pausing for a moment, he continued, "By the way, how is that new Seaman Smith of yours, the one you picked up in Santos?"

This was the first opportunity I had had to discuss Walter Smith with an understanding, sympathetic person. I replied:

> Seaman Smith is an enigma to me. First of all, he is a member of the

Regular U.S. Navy, not of the U.S. Naval Reserve, as are most of the others. I was asked by local authorities in Santos to take him back to the States. He had been in jail in Brazil for street fighting, although his papers say he was hospitalized. He is the most experienced member of my crew . . . but also the most unpredictable. He is, as you must know, the only one who carries a long hunting knife in a sheath on his belt. This bothers me, especially if he is inclined to get into personal fights. I have warned him about the dangers of carrying a knife . . . but I have not taken it away from him. Frankly, I feel somewhat embarrassed with my crew by seeming to be ambivalent — is that the word? — in my treatment of Smith. So far I have chosen to ignore the knife . . . but I may take it from him when he goes ashore in foreign ports.

After some minutes Chief Chalk broached another subject.

Do you realize that we are now approaching the very waters where three small British cruisers engaged the German "pocket battleship" *Graf Spee* in December 1939?

Although I was reasonably familiar with the story, I encouraged him to continue. He did.

It was the first significant battle of the war after Germany had conquered Poland in September. It was a classic naval engagement . . . one which the British Admiralty had anticipated and developed tactics for, years before the war.

Graf Spee was one of Germany's prewar secrets — a "pocket battleship" class vessel of a reported 10,000 tons, carrying six 11-inch guns, and believed to have armour-plated steel hull and decks. She slipped out of German waters before the war started, and spent the first three months of the war attacking British merchant ships on both sides of the South Atlantic.

The British battleships were being held in reserve with the Home Fleet at Scapa Flow, intended to protect the British Isles and the Western Approaches for convoys from possible attack by other German capital ships. Only four light cruisers were available to pursue *Graf Spee* in the South Atlantic, under command of Commodore Henry Harwood. His instructions were very explicit: If one or two of his small-gunned, but fast, cruisers were to encounter *Graf Spee*, they were to avoid an engagement but maintain contact and advise the Admiralty by radio. If three or four of the cruisers were to encounter the German ship they were to seek an engagement, using tactics which had been carefully developed.

On the morning of 13 December 1939, Commander Harwood and three light cruisers — HMS *Exeter*, HMS *Ajax* and HMNZS *Achilles*, the latter under New Zealand command — were patroling off the mouth of Rio de la Plata. A fourth cruiser, HMS *Cumberland*, was being refitted in the Falkland Islands, 1,500 miles to the south.

When *Graf Spee*, also operating off Rio de la Plata, spotted the three British ships, she initially identified them as destroyers, not expecting to meet three cruisers in company. She immediately sought an engagement and was soon encircled by the three British warships before she realized they were cruisers.

In the 36-hour running engagement which ensued, *Graf Spee* succeeded in knocking out, but not sinking, the *Exeter*, the largest cruiser and Harwood's flagship. Meanwhile, by successfully maneuvering with the use of smokescreens, *Ajax* and *Achilles* with their smaller six-inch guns succeeded in inflicting serious damage to *Graf Spee*.

On 15 December, Captain Hans Langsdorff in *Graf Spee* took his damaged ship, with dead and wounded crewmen, into the neutral port of Montevideo. His object was to gain enough time to bury his dead, repair his ship, and return to the action.

However, an international diplomatic crisis ensued, in which the Uruguayan government was persuaded by the British to limit *Graf Spee*'s time in port. Captain Langsdorff radioed Germany for instructions and was personally ordered by Hitler to scuttle his ship rather than have it interned in Uruguay.

On 17 December, with thousands of Uruguayans watching on the shore, and the whole world listening by radio, Langsdorff moved *Graf Spee* out into Rio de la Plata and blew it up. Later in Buenos Aires, he committed suicide.

Subsequently, more than 1,000 German Naval personnel were interned in neutral Argentina. They have been there now for nearly five years. There is a large German colony in Buenos Aires. Only the Lord knows what mischief may have been afoot there since 1939.

Having completed his long monologue in British pride, Chief Mate Chalk paused briefly, then said, "I'm going to turn in. Don't call me for the Punta del Este light. I have to go back on watch at 0400. Good night."

After Chief Mate Chalk had left, I walked over to the starboard wing of the bridge, looked up at the stars, and began to reminisce to myself about my experiences of the past several months, which were so foreign to my previous humdrum Hoosier habits.

At 10 p.m. I was awakened from my reveries by "four bells" — midway in the watch. I left the bridge, walked along the main deck to the bow- and stern-gun tubs, and visited with the Navy gunners on duty. In the great confidence and optimism of youth, the Navy boys seemed totally oblivious to possible U-boat attack and were only interested in what kind of a liberty port Montevideo would be, meaning "bars and babes."

Returning to the midship house, I looked into the crew mess hall, where Merchant and Navy seamen were drinking coffee, eating cold-cut sandwiches, playing cards, and regaling each other with stories of uncertain veracity regarding their own experiences at sea and ashore.

At one table, playing "Acey-Deucey," were Bosun Hobbs, a Black, and Chow Sung, the Chinese cook. As senior but minority members of the crew, they shared a cabin and were close friends.

At around 11 p.m., I decided to go down into the engine room to visit my shipboard friend, First Assistant Engineer Walter F. Miller, of Racine, Wisconsin, then off watch but in charge of an overtime maintenance crew. Walter and his boss, Chief Engineer Seaberg, had often chided me that I spent too much time on the bridge with the Captain and mates and never visited them in the engine room.

Walter and I had become friends quite easily. We were both about 30, both from Midwestern backgrounds, and both far from our youthful environments. Our principal difference was the fact that, during the war, he had become a maritime engineer while I hardly knew a nut from a bolt.

Only *half* jokingly, Walter and Chief Engineer Seaberg had attributed my aloofness to an apparent reluctance on my part to soil my uniform with grease in the engine room. Actually, they *knew*, as I did, that I was suffering from a kind of landlubber's claustrophobia — a fear of being below the water line when the ship was at sea, especially at night. Everyone recognized, without commenting on it, that a torpedo striking amidships would almost certainly wipe out the entire engineering crew then on watch.

With more self-confidence than I actually possessed, I gingerly negotiated the steel ladders and catwalks, running inside the ship from the main deck to the engine room, which was in the noisy, cavernous bowels of the vessel.

Actually surprised at my appearance below decks, Walter greeted me aloud, for the benefit of his crew and to the amusement of his oilers and wipers.

"Well, the Navy lieutenant has finally discovered where we work."

The engine room crew, then as always, was drinking black coffee, which was brought to them continuously from the ship's galley by the junior oiler or wiper then on watch. Walter offered me coffee in a used mug, which I declined. Since Santos, the ship's brew had seemed pretty foul stuff.

Always an engineer, Walter proceeded to explain to me that the ship was then making 9.5 knots in a calm sea. The temperature of the air was then only a few degrees colder than the temperature of the sea water, which meant that the engine was operating efficiently.

I was interested, but *not* to the point of taking notes, as I occasionally looked upward to the high upper bulkheads and found myself speculating as to how far below the water line we were standing.

Finally, perhaps seeking an excuse for a short visit, I told Walter that I wanted to go up to the "radio shack" on the bridge deck to hear the midnight short-wave radio broadcast of the day's war dispatches from the BBC in London.

In the previous months I had been at sea, the midnight BBC reports had become a last ritual of each day. Having no newspapers or other means of communication aboard, the BBC had become virtually the sole source of war information to Allied ships at sea or in foreign ports.

Aboard *William Gaston*, I had also become friendly with "Sparks," Radio Operator Foreman Lester Godown, who served an important but rather lonely function aboard ship. Unlike the deck and engineering departments, which had officers and crews for each watch, Radio Operator Godown had a one-man schedule. He was on watch in the "radio shack" nearly 18 hours a day and, of course, was subject to call at all times.

At midnight on 3 July 1944, Lester and I sat together in his small office on the bridge deck, port side aft, and listened by radio to the tolling of Big Ben, followed by the somber voice saying, "This is the BBC . . . calling from London. . . ."

On that particular occasion . . . more than 1,750 nights since the war had started in September 1939, the crisp-voiced British announcer reported, unemotionally:

> Today, on the continent, Allied Armed Forces, supported by fighter and bomber aircraft, continued to drive German armies out of Northern France. . . .
>
> The U.S. 12th Army Group under General Omar Bradley is forcing the Germans from St. Lo on the Contentin Peninsula. . . . The British 21st Army Group, under Field Marshal Montgomery, is attacking to the East near Caen. . . . The military roads to Paris are being opened. . . .
>
> The Admiralty announced today that another large trans-Atlantic Allied convoy from the United States and Canada has safely arrived at ports in the United Kingdom without loss of a single merchant or naval ship. . . .
>
> In the East, the Russian armies are continuing their advance into Poland and have started shelling the German garrison in Warsaw. . . .
>
> In Italy, the multi-nation Allied Forces are encountering stiff German resistance in the North, South of Florence. . . .

In the Pacific, the U.S. Fleet and Air Forces continued to shell and bomb the Japanese-held island of Guam in preparation for an invasion expected later this Summer. . . .

We close this broadcast on a somber note from the home front. During recent days, German rocket bombs have continued to fall on London and the British Isles. Today Prime Minister Churchill announced that during recent raids, 10,752 Londoners have died in explosions of these "secret weapons" of Herr Hitler. . . ."

Soon after midnight I returned to the bridge, just in time to hear a report from a Navy seaman in the forward-gun tub that a flashing light was visible on the starboard bow, about five miles distant. Surely it was Punte del Este light.

Third Mate Howard Carandee, then Officer of the Watch, sent a seaman to call Captain Chase, who soon joined us in the wheel house. Through binoculars we could all see the light growing brighter until we finally passed it on our starboard side.

Finally, Captain Chase gave an order to change course 45° to starboard. We were entering the estuary of the Rio de la Plata. Although no one commented on it, we were all privately relieved, as we knew that the river delta was too shallow for U-boats to operate.

Suddenly I became very tired. I decided to go to bed and, as my Irish father used to say, "dream of tomorrow's sport."

Two views of the German "pocket battleship" *Graf Spee.* Above: At the pier in Montevideo, Uruguay, December 1939, awaiting repairs to the damage sustained in an engagement with British cruisers. Below: The *Graf Spee* being blown up in Rio de la Plata by her crew after sailing from Montevideo. The wreckage was visible for years because of shallow water in the river. (UPI Wirephotos)

Chapter 7

Montevideo, Uruguay — July 1944

On 4 July, Independence Day back in the States, *William Gaston* tied up at a pier in Montevideo, having earlier sailed past the wreckage of *Graf Spee*, whose superstructure was clearly visible in the shallow La Plata River nearly five years after its disasterous scuttling. At a nearby pier in the port, the German freighter *Tacoma*, supply ship to the German "pocket battleship," was still tied up after having been interned in December 1939.

While our ship was discharging her cargo of machinery and auto and truck tires, the Merchant and Navy crews had opportunities to see the colorful capital of the small, prosperous South American republic. After the United States had been drawn into the war in December 1941, Uruguay had broken diplomatic relations with the Axis powers, and the people of Montevideo were very courteous to their neighbors from the North.

As a fairly typical *Norte Americano* from the Midwest, I had assumed that little Uruguay was a small, underdeveloped country. I was amazed to find that Montevideo was an impressive modern city, with great architecture, wide *avenidas* and beautiful parks. I was especially awed by the luxurious gambling casino, the first I had ever seen, which seemed to me a monument to wealth and sophistication.

According to history or legend, take your choice, Montevideo was given its name by a sailor on a sixteenth century Portuguese ship of exploration. As the ship passed near the coast of what is now Uruguay, the seaman on watch reportedly shouted, "*montevideo, montevideo,*" meaning "I see a mountain."

Actually the sailor was guilty of some exaggeration. The mountain was less than 400 feet in elevation, and to this day is known locally as *el cerro*, "the hill." In 1944, it was most noteworthy because of an old fort, located at the top, which fired a cannon once a day to signal 12 o'clock noon.

Another point of interest to North Americans was a large equestrian statue of a South American *gaucho* in the Plazuela Lorenzo Justiniano Perez. The *gaucho* is the counterpart of the North American cowboy. Because of the importance of cattle raising in some South American countries, the *gauchos* enjoy a kind of affection and esteem which North American cowboys never attained, except in the movies, of course.

Although it was mid-winter in the Southern Hemisphere, the Uruguayan capital was temperate and beautiful. We saw many of the tourist sights and met friendly people in bars and restaurants. The waterfront operations seemed more efficient than those in Brazil, and as a result, we unfortunately spent only a few days there discharging the other half of our cargo.

Captain Chase, Chief Mate Chalk, and Chief Engineer Seaberg were kept busy with the ship's in-port business, but we were able to have dinner ashore each evening.

The Merchant and Navy crews were reluctant at the prospect of early sailing. They were finding Montevideo a great liberty port, and they went ashore at every opportunity. Returning late at night, they were filled with age-old sailors' tales of "bars and babes." And the prices were right too!

While in Montevideo, in a replay of Santos, I met in a restaurant a winsome young girl in her twenties. She told me that she was Cuban and that her name was Suzie. Fortunately, she could speak pretty fair English, and we were able to establish a kind of friendship even if on a wartime, here-today-gone-tomorrow basis.

On two occasions, Suzie took time off from the dress shop where she worked. We went sightseeing around Montevideo and even attended an American movie. She told me she was embarrassed to be seen with a man in uniform as that indicated the nature of our relationship. As a courtesy to her, I removed all Navy insignia from my khaki cap, shirt, and jacket — which, fortunately, was never noted in my Navy Fitness Report!

* * *

Although smoking has never been one of my favorite vices, I was at that time buying an occasional package of American cigarettes from the ship's "slop chest" operated by the purser, Marshall Edward Maxwell.

One day, while strolling around Montevideo, I decided to have a smoke but discovered I had no matches. I stopped an Uruguayan gentleman on the sidewalk, acted out the process of striking a match on a box, and, drawing upon my miniscule Spanish vocabulary, said *"fosforo, fosforo."*

Imagine my chagrin when he smiled and replied, "Whattsa matter Mac? Ya wanna match?"

* * *

On the morning of 7 July, pursuant to our orders, we prepared to proceed up La Plata and Paraña Rivers to Rosario, Argentina's large inland city, to load corn for return delivery to the United States. Iowa farmers would have been amazed! A-maized?

In the early afternoon *William Gaston* cast off from Montevideo and headed up river to Rosario, nearly 350 miles into the interior of Argentina. After long earlier weeks at sea, with no sights to be seen except horizons, a river passage through the lush Pampas plains of Argentina was to be a real thrill for this sailor/tourist from Indiana.

Chapter 8

Rosario, Argentina

After an upstream passage of two days and nights, *William Gaston* on 9 July tied up at a grain-loading pier in the port of Rosario, Argentina's second biggest city and second-most important seaport after the capital, Buenos Aires.

Rosario had very modern port facilities, with railheads to receive carloads of corn and wheat at the waterfront from *estancias* in the interior, and a row of huge grain elevators on the docks to load cargo ships very efficiently.

With a population of about 500,000, Rosario was a flourishing city, which served as more than the hub of an important Argentine agricultural center and a major port for the country's export trade. It was also an important railway center, being the mid-point between Buenos Aires and Cordoba for two separate rail lines — one narrow gauge and one broad gauge. Each had stations in Rosario, which could only be described as nineteenth century ornate.

Upon arrival at Rosario, it had soon become apparent that the Argentina government was, as we had heard, "neutral but pro-Axis." To quote from my U.S. Naval Armed Guard Report:

The observance of Argentine neutrality imposed certain restrictions which warrant mention: Briefly, it was necessary either to seal under Argentine bond or declare before Argentine customs, virtually every article aboard the vessel, whether personally owned or owned by the War Shipping Administration, the ship's owner; American West African Lines, the ship's operator; or the U.S. Navy. It was necessary to declare the ship's armament (in non-technical language only), to place all ammunition under seal, and to stand security watches without sidearms — all of which was approved by the U.S. Naval Attache.

Nevertheless, Rosario proved a very agreeable place, with an ambience, an architecture, and a lifestyle somewhat reminiscent of the smaller seaport of Santos, Brazil. The people around the waterfront were friendly, and they were interested in Argentine grain exports to the United States. However, unlike Santos, we did not have the good offices of an American shipping agent like James Bacon, and our social contacts were limited to the *Rosariños* we met in local bars and restaurants. There were, however, two seaman's missions operated by Catholic and Protestant churches, at which American sailors were welcome.

As I recall, we took trolley cars from the waterfront to the center of Rosario, where we strolled along Calle San Martin with its impressive rows of public buildings, hotels, apartments, bars, restaurants, and banks, where we could exchange U.S. dollars for Argentine pesos.

If my principal impressions of Santos included *good coffee*, in Rosario they were the great *beefsteak* and "free lunches" of abundant Argentine food at every bar — a custom which had long since disappeared in the U.S.

As I recall, a steak dinner with all the "extras" cost about 75 cents in U.S. currency. However, *one* of the Argentine extras was a fried egg on top of the steak, the soft yolk of which was regarded as a kind of steak sauce. In spite of my limitations with foreign languages, I soon learned a few words of Spanish so I could order steak *without the egg*!

We really enjoyed our several days in Rosario. It was a prosperous and happy city and seemed wonderfully remote from the realities of the war. The climate was mild for mid-winter, food and drinks were abundant and inexpensive, and the people were friendly. It was the sort of place any sailor would have been happy to settle down "for the duration," assuming he could overcome homesickness.

It never entered my mind that we were under observation throughout the whole of our stay. Years later, I learned from Argentine sources that Dr. Wolf Meissner, a distinguished German gentleman spy, who was the head of a Nazi ring in Rosario, helped by a team of volunteers, made it a practice to identify the grain ships among all the foreign-flag vessels tied up in the port of Rosario. The ships were photographed from every angle, their silhouettes imprinted on millimeter graph paper to aid nighttime identification; and, in the thick tangle of green of the islands on the far side of the Paraña, powerful binoculars were trained on all allied ships to note the movements of their crews.

While in Rosario, an idea occurred to me that some American businessmen located there might be willing to provide a little hospitality to our U.S. Navy crew members, who didn't have much spending money and, in spite of local friendliness, were not very comfortable in a strange city. With the assistance of an English-speaking telephone operator, I was able to get in touch with the American manager of Frigorifico Swift & Company of Chicago. He said he and his associates would be delighted to host a barbecue picnic for us. The next morning they picked us up at the dock in American cars and drove us out to an *estancia* outside the city, where we played softball, drank beer, and ate *empañadas* and barbecued beef. It was a memorable day, far from home.

Unfortunately, I have been unable to recall or to obtain from Swift in Chicago the names of our gracious hosts.

Almost regrettably, we were advised that *William Gaston* would complete two-thirds of its cargo loading on 12 July and would proceed downstream to "top off" at Buenos Aires, the world-famous "Paris of America," which we were all eager to visit.

Chapter 9

Buenos Aires, Argentina

On Friday, 14 July, *William Gaston* was tied up at another grain-loading pier on Rio de la Plata in the port of Buenos Aires, which we had reached the previous evening. We were moored parallel to the main dock, headed downstream, where we had a close-up, 24 hour-a-day view of the considerable traffic on La Plata.

Because of the relatively shallow depth of Argentine rivers, it was the practice to partially load departing freighters with corn or wheat at Rosario and to "top off" down river at Buenos Aires. Even with this precaution, *William Gaston* had scraped her propeller on the river bottom between the two ports and faced the prospect of extensive repairs at Buenos Aires.

As we were tying up in twilight on 13 July at the river wharf in the Argentine capital, we became aware that we were entering an exciting new world. Whereas the major cities of the warring powers were then blacked out at night, neutral Buenos Aires was brightly lit, almost festive in aspect.

And, whereas Santos and Rosario had been relatively modest maritime ports, Buenos Aires was a huge, sophisticated, beautiful, bustling metropolitan city of more than 3,000,000.

After the docking procedures, it was too late for our crew's liberty that night, but everyone on *William Gaston* looked forward to seeing the local sights in the following days.

It was mid-winter in the Southern Hemisphere. The weather in Buenos Aires was cold and damp, but not freezing. Situated at about 30° South latitude — roughly comparable to the Carolinas in the United States. The Argentine capital experienced milder winters than most major cities in North America.

Early in the morning of 14 July, Lieutenant-Commander C.W. Finstrom, USNR, of the U.S. Naval Attaché's Office at the American Embassy in

Buenos Aires, came aboard *William Gaston*. He welcomed us to the Argentine capital, reviewed for us our restrictions in observance of Argentine neutrality, and gave the usual advice that crew members should avoid certain neighborhoods in the city, *i.e.*, the red light districts.

That type of advice was always counterproductive. It simply made it easier for the seamen to find those areas! Finstrom also explained that there was a large German colony in Buenos Aires and that we might encounter some anti-American sentiment. He advised us to be discreet and mind our own business, avoiding any public behavior which might worsen matters. I called a meeting of the gun crew to review those instructions, and at its conclusion, I called Seaman Walter Smith aside and asked him not to wear his hunting knife when he went ashore. He readily agreed.

After setting up in-port watches for the gun crew, I went ashore with First Engineer Walter Miller to do some sightseeing in Buenos Aires. We still had Argentine pesos, which we had picked up in Rosario. Walter and I were able to hire a taxi near the waterfront, and we asked the driver to show us the sights of the city. If we had been impressed with the size and beauty of Montevideo, we were literally overwhelmed by the grandeur of Buenos Aires. Most North Americans of that period had no concept of the splendor of South American capital cities. In the United States, New York City was a great seaport and commercial center; Washington, D.C., was the seat of government. In Argentina, Buenos Aires was both. To most Americans, New York City meant the Island of Manhattan, where, because of land limitations, the city had always grown upward rather than outward, with narrow streets, high-rise buildings, and few large open spaces, except Central Park. By contrast, Washington then had, and still has, wide avenues, impressive government buildings, and a feeling of openness. Buenos Aires combined aspects of both New York and Washington — lots of commercial bustle but softened by wide *avenidas*, ornate government buildings, and even palm trees.

Fortunately, our taxi driver spoke pretty fair English, and he was able to describe many of the buildings and monuments we saw in central Buenos Aires. I remember, in particular, the Presidential Palace, Casa Rosada, known as "The Pink House" — in contrast to the American White House. I also remember Avenida 9 de Julio, which, with its ten lanes of traffic, was reputed to be the widest boulevard of any city in the world.

Around midday our driver dropped us off near Calle Florida, one of Buenos Aires' world-famous shopping streets, which was sometimes closed to vehicular traffic and converted into a pedestrian mall. While my memory of this detail is not too clear, I seem to recall that the custom was known locally as something like "footie-footie." The shops on Calle Florida were comparable to those on Fifth Avenue in New York City, and even in wartime were stocked with luxurious merchandise. As a kind of Yankee tourist and souvenir hunter, I was particularly impressed with beautiful ladies' purses, made of unborn calfskin, and bought several to take home to Indiana.

Early in the afternoon Walter and I stopped into a cafe for lunch — Scotch whisky, grilled beef steaks, and great Argentine beer. Then we decided to walk back to the ship. En route, for the first time, we became aware that there *were* anti-American elements in the local populace. In our U.S. military uniforms we were abused verbally several times and spit at by other pedestrians. In researching for this book, I have been assured by both American residents there and Argentine people that most Buenos Aires *porteños* were supporters of the Allied powers, but all admit that there *were* pro-Axis factions in the Argentine population, even in high places in the government.

That evening Captain Chase, Chief Mate Chalk, Chief Engineer Seaberg, and I strolled up to a nearby waterfront cafe known as Ta-Ba-Ris, to have dinner and enjoy the local nightlife. Ta-Ba-Ris was a better-than-average South American waterfront bistro compared to what we had seen in Santos, Montevideo, and Rosario. It was obviously intended to cater to the interests of visiting Navy and Merchant Marine officers, with drinks of all kinds, good hearty food, music, dancing, entertainers, and attractive hostesses. It was, as an Argentine friend later told me, "*not* the sort of place to which a married man would take his wife."

One of my principal recollections about the place was that the dancing was a participant activity for a limited number of patrons, but a spectator sport for everyone else. The local Argentine men danced the tango beautifully with either their girlfriends or the hostesses. The visiting American maritime officers had the good sense not to try to foxtrot to tango music.

Scotch whisky and English gin were abundant and inexpensive at Ta-Ba-Ris, as were the Argentine steaks. The *William Gaston* officers had a surfeit of both. In those days I could, and did, eat steak two or three times a day.

One of my fondest memories of Ta-Ba-Ris involves an attractive Argentine woman who was about thirty and a vocalist with the orchestra. One of her popular numbers was a haunting tango entitled "Uno." With my Irish courage bolstered by Scotch whisky, I asked the owner-manager to bring her to our table for a drink. He kindly obliged. Her name was Maria. She was very friendly with our group, but she spoke very little English, and our incipient friendship encountered a serious language barrier.

Sometime after midnight, the *William Gaston* officers walked leisurely back to the ship, having become, so we thought, real Buenos Aires *porteños*. We were aware that our ship had a possibly damaged propeller and that we might be delayed for repairs. Frankly, that was not a discouraging prospect.

* * *

Since arriving in Buenos Aires on 13 July, we had learned that *William*

Gaston was the first U.S. Merchant ship to have called there in some time, and it was obvious that we were attracting some unusual attention on the waterfront. Although we really didn't understand it at the time, it was apparent that Buenos Aires was much more *politicized* than our previous ports of call — Santos, Montevideo, and Rosario. The U.S. Navy crew continued to enjoy its shore leaves in the Argentine capital, but our American uniforms were inviting more public notice than we wanted, and we had had additional experiences in being abused verbally by some pedestrians on the street.

Chief Engineer Seaberg and I had one of the more surprising and unpleasant experiences. On a Saturday evening we had attended an opera performance at the beautiful Teatro Colon and were openly hissed inside and in front of the opera house by some members of the formally dressed audience.

Nevertheless, during the days, we continued our sightseeing in Buenos Aires, and, in the evenings, checked out the nightlife of the colorful capital. In maritime tradition, of course, the officers and men frequented different establishments.

For the *William Gaston* crew, one of the "pluses" of Buenos Aires was the fact that we had access for the first time in several months to an English-language newspaper — the 100-year-old *Buenos Aires Herald*, a tabloid-sized paper, owned and published by British interests. The *Herald* enabled us to keep up with important developments in the war, from which we seemed so far removed. It also helped us to get some feeling for the local wartime lifestyle in Buenos Aires. The paper included thorough coverage of Argentine soccer and horse racing and an amazing amount of advertising and publicity for relatively current American movies. The *Herald* also carried daily reports of arrivals and departures of neutral Spanish and Argentine passenger ships, and the arrivals and departures, by personal names, of travelers on Panagra and Condor international airlines.

At one of the waterfront bars frequented by seamen, someone had clipped and posted a front-page story from the *Herald* of 20 February 1944, carrying the banner headline, "SPIES BY SUBMARINE!" It reported that two new German agents and some cargo had been landed by rubber boat from a U-boat off Mar del Plata on the Atlantic coast of Argentina. The same sub reportedly picked up for return to Germany four or five other Nazi agents then being sought by Argentine police.

One of my recollections of Buenos Aires is the fact that virtually every retail store seemed to be featuring window displays of Scotch whisky and British gin, which were relatively scarce in 1944 in most other parts of the world. Apparently the English were trading those exports in exchange for Argentine beef and grains. Needless to say, the crew of *William Gaston* found whisky and gin to be among the most attractive of Argentine souvenirs.

For the Merchant crew in nondescript seamen's clothing, Buenos Aires was

Buenos Aires Herald

BUENOS AIRES, SUNDAY, FEBRUARY 20, 1944.

SPIES BY SUBMARINE

COAST OF Bs. As. PROVINCE SURVEYED BY NAZI SPIES

First Police Report on Local Espionage Activities

THE amazing revelation that Major General Freidrich Wolf, Military and Naval Attache to the German Embassy, had commissioned one of his underlings, Guillermo Otto Seidlitz, to survey the coast of the province of Buenos Aires for the purpose of finding a convenient spot for landing two spies, their luggage and equipment, from a German submarine was made in a statement on German espionage activities given out by the Federal Police yesterday.

The front page of the *Buenos Aires Herald*, 20 February 1944. The headline reveals the Argentine police report of local Nazi spy activity. At the right is a photo of a *quinto*, or country house, located in Bella Vista, which was used by the spies as a photo laboratory to duplicate documents for sending to Germany, and which had been recently raided by Argentine police. (Library of Congress, Washington, D.C.)

a very agreeable port of call, and they were eager to go ashore daily and nightly between in-port duties aboard ship.

Buenos Aires proved an especially pleasant interlude for Black Bosun Alonzo Hobbs and Chinese Chief Cook Chow Sung, who had become good friends. Aboard ship each carried the dual burden of being members of a minority in America and also of being supervisor of less-experienced Caucasians, who resented them. By contrast, while ashore, they blended easily into the international community of the Buenos Aires waterfront.

One night, when returning to the ship after an evening at a seaman's bar, Hobbs and Sung chanced upon a stray mongrel dog wandering along the pier. Although it was against the rules, they decided to sneak the dog aboard ship and give it some food, which Sung could readily obtain from the ship's galley. Later, on an unwise but well-meaning impulse, the two men decided to keep the dog on board, planning to conceal it from Captain Chase by hiding it in the Bosun's paint locker during daylight and at night bringing it into the double-bunked stateroom, which they shared on the main deck. Eventually, the men decided to give the dog a name, and even in this they reached a unique harmony. Because the dog had been picked up in Argentina, Bosun Hobbs preferred a Spanish name and called the dog *Juan*. Chief Cook Sung agreed. He called it *Wan*.

On the whole, the experience of *William Gaston* officers and crew in Buenos Aires were always interesting and only occasionally unpleasant.

* * *

On Tuesday, 18 July, *William Gaston* was still tied up at the loading pier of the grain elevator and the "topping off" of Argentine corn was nearly completed, when Captain Chase received orders from the U.S. Naval Attaché that we were to sail on 19 July, routed independently to Rio de Janeiro, to join a U.S. Navy convoy bound for Trinidad and then to an unannounced U.S. port.

In the previous days, underwater divers had inpsected the ship's propeller, reporting to Captain Chase and Chief Engineer Seaberg that the blades were scraped but not bent, that the driveshaft appeared to be undamaged, and that the ship could sail without repairs. We were almost disappointed!

With only one evening remaining, the *William Gaston* senior officers and I decided to have a farewell dinner at Ta-Ba-Ris, which had become our "headquarters" in Buenos Aires. By that time our group, as virtually the only American visitors on the waterfront, had become well recognized by the owner-manager, bartenders, waiters, and entertainers at the cabaret. On previous evenings we had always invited Maria to join us at our table. We all enjoyed a bit of feminine company, although our language barrier precluded any real communication.

During earlier visits I had become attracted to the young Argentine woman and was trying to carry on a little flirtation with her. She knew that I loved the song "Uno" and always sang it after we had arrived. In fact, I had already purchased a locally produced 78 rpm record of the song to add to my Argentine souvenirs.

Unforntunately, my flirtation with Maria was getting nowhere, mainly, I thought, because of the language barrier. At closing time each night I was limited to saying, *"Buenos noches*, Maria." I simply lacked the experience and sophistication to suggest whatever the Argentines considered "a date" in a big, strange city like Buenos Aires.

The evening of Tuesday, 18 July, was even more festive than usual. Everyone in the place seemed to know that the American ship was sailing in the morning, which was in violation of all wartime cautions against revealing ship movements. The cabaret was crowded with Argentine, British, and Spanish officers from other ships in port.

Between her floor-show appearances, Maria joined us at the table. Perhaps because it was to be our farewell, I finally got up the courage to hold one of her hands between us under the table. And, as millions of other young couples have experienced, that touch expressed far more than our awkward attempts at conversation.

Between shows, in the traditional camaraderie among seamen, several Argentine, British, and Spanish merchant officers visited our table for handshakes and a few friendly words in their languages. In turn, Captain Chase, Chief Mate Chalk, and Chief Engineer Seaberg visited other tables to toast the others and try to express goodwill. Captain Chase and Chief Mate Chalk spoke only English. Chief Engineer Seaberg could also speak Swedish, but there were none of his compatriots in the cabaret.

Maria and I welcomed the absences of the *William Gaston* officers as that gave us more privacy for our hand holding. Still unable to converse, except superficially in our native tongues, we discovered that we could communicate to some degree by humming together the haunting melody of "Uno."

I still remember Maria's lovely black hair and brown eyes, which framed and highlighted her clear Castilian complexion. I wished the evening would never end. I wasn't even looking forward to sailing for home the following morning. When the time came to leave, Maria excused herself to pick up her wrap in the dressing room. But this time I went to the front door to await her return. There was a wordless exchange of understanding. I took her hand again and we walked outside, where she led me to a waiting taxi and gave the driver instructions in Spanish.

As I recall, we were driven to a small apartment building or duplex in a residential neighborhood about a mile from the cabaret. While I allowed the driver to take his fare from my Argentine pesos, Maria used her own key to open the door, leading to a stairway to the second floor. Once inside I found that our language barrier was no longer a problem but an actual advantage. We didn't try to speak at first. I simply took her in my arms and kissed her gently but for a long time.

Inside her bedroom, she allowed me to remove her shoes and dress, after which I took off my own outer clothing and guided her to the double bed. Then, to my consternation and annoyance, she began to speak emotionally in a melange of Spanish and English. She asked me if I had ever heard of Eva Duarte. I indicated I had not.

She told me that "Eva . . . some call her Evita . . . is *la compañera* to Colonel Juan Peron, who is now *el Vice Presidente de Los Argentinas.*"

I mumbled "*si, si,*" but really meant "so what?"

Then Maria launched into a Spanish-English monologue.

"I am like Evita. She, too was a singer-actress in Buenos Aires. Like her, my father is *un estanciero rico*. He is married . . . but not to my mother. Some call me *una huacha* [nest egg] *Por que*? *Porque soy hija natural*, [natural daughter] *Que culpa tengo yo? Yo no hice nada malo* [nothing bad]."

She then broke down and sobbed softly. I was touched with compassion as I rarely have been in my life. I remembered something I had read somewhere and tried to explain it to her in English.

"Someone has written 'There are no illegitimate children, only illegitimate parents,' " I said.

Then, totally at a loss for words which would mean anything to Maria, I took her into my arms, whispered "*Uno, Uno*" into her ear, kissed her again, and tried to comfort her in her deep unhappiness.

Later, she asked me if I was married, which didn't surprise me. I told her I was not, which was the truth. Then, strangely, she asked me about the other men on our ship. Were they married? Did they have wives and children in *Norte America*? I told her I thought some of them did, but I couldn't understand her concern. At the time I attributed it to her own broken family life.

When I left her at daybreak, Maria seemed genuinely affectionate when she kissed me goodbye, saying "*Adios, mi Yanqui amigo. Que Dios te guarde* [may God protect you]."

As I walked back to the waterfront and to *William Gaston*, I watched the sun rising in the east, bringing a new day to bustling Buenos Aires. In spite of a few early unpleasantnesses, I had really enjoyed the Argentine capital. I knew I would miss Maria for awhile, but I realized that the chances of my ever seeing her again were most remote.

Still, I was puzzled about her apparent concern for the wives and children of our crew members. It was later, much later, when I finally realized that Maria may have known something about *William Gaston* that I didn't know.

It was then about 6:30 a.m., Wednesday, 19 July 1944.

Chapter 10

Homeward Bound — 19 July 1944

Boarding *William Gaston* at the pier at about 7 a.m., I first went to my stateroom to change from "dress blues" into "shipboard khakis," then to the Navy crew quarters to ascertain that all hands were on board. I then had breakfast in the officers' wardroom, and finally went to the bridge, which was already stirring with the duties of the parting ship.

William Gaston cast off lines at about 9 a.m. and started down the Rio de la Plata. Crewmen without more pressing duties lined the starboard rail for one final view of Buenos Aires.

As we sailed down the estuary, we noted that a small coastal freighter seemed to be following us rather closely. We attached no particular significance to it at the time, as there was a fair amount of other ships' traffic on the river, headed both upstream and downstream.

During the afternoon we had had another look at the wreckage of *Graf Spee* as we passed her close abeam off Montevideo. The 1939 German commerce raider of the Atlantic was then a rusting hulk, her superstructure still visible above the waves.

At around 4 p.m., as we reached the open sea, we were surprised to note that the small ship had altered her course just as we had and had taken up a position about one mile off our starboard quarter. Through binoculars, we could see that she was flying the blue-and-white flag of Argentina. Captain Chase observed that she was a coastal freighter of about 200 tons, and that, judging from the dark smoke from her stack, she was probably a coal burner.

At sunset, during general quarters, we were further surprised when the small Argentine ship turned on her running lights for the night. As a neutral vessel, that was proper procedure for her. However, it seemed strange to the *William Gaston* crew, as most of us had never seen a neutral ship at sea before.

Among the ship's crew there was considerable discussion about the identity and probable destination of the other vessel. Most of us assumed that she was a legitimate neutral, probably headed for a Brazilian port, and therefore on a course parallel to ours.

However, during the 8 to 12 watch, Second Mate Pennino, acting on Captain Chase's orders, made several minor changes of course. After each of these, the mate checked the relative bearing of the Argentine vessel through the azimuth viewer on the ship's flying bridge and found the other ship was making course changes exactly the same as those of *William Gaston*.

Second Mate Pennino reported this to the Captain, who sent a seaman to my stateroom with a request that I join the watch on the bridge. We talked for some minutes about the unusual behavior of the Argentinian, but concluded that there was nothing we could do about it. As a Merchant ship ourselves, we had no authority to use our blinker light to ask the other ship to identify herself. Besides, no one on *William Gaston* could speak Spanish, and it seemed unlikely that anyone on such a small Argentine ship would speak English.

In retrospect, it was theoretically possible for us to send a radio signal to U.S. or Allied Naval authorities in Uruguay or Brazil, reporting that we were being pursued. However, we had been expressly instructed not to break radio silence during our passage to Rio.

At length, as I recall, the Captain said something like, "The damn fools probably don't know how to navigate and are simply following us to Rio!"

With that, the Captain left the bridge, saying he was going down to the wardroom to have several cups of black coffee, which he did every night as he said it helped him to get to sleep!

By daybreak on the second day out of Buenos Aires, *William Gaston* had sailed nearly 300 sea miles down the Rio de la Plata and out into the South Atlantic and was then steering a northeasterly course toward Rio de Janeiro, speed 8.5 knots.

During our first two days out the crew had settled down to its usual shipboard routines after nearly three weeks ashore in three different ports. The morale of both Merchant and Navy crews was very good, as we were homeward bound for the first time in nearly three months since sailing from New York. Adding to the good morale was the fact that the ship's meals were the best in weeks, as we had taken on fresh stores of meat, vegetables, and fruit in Argentina.

The mid-winter weather on off-shore South America was even milder than it had been in Buenos Aires. The coastline to the west was capped with scattered cumulus clouds. There was a mild breeze blowing out of the southwest, causing a moderate sea swell to follow *William Gaston*. The skies

The *Besugo*, the small Argentine coastal freighter which followed the *William Gaston* out of Buenos Aires and tracked it for five days and nights in July 1944. Forty years later, the author learned that the *Besugo* was owned and operated by a shipping line which had been "blacklisted" by the Allies because of "pro-Axis activities." (Photo courtesy of Argentine Archives)

were clear on the first night out, and we could watch the Southern Cross gradually sinking toward the horizon in the wake we were leaving in the slowly rolling seas and silent night.

As usual, on the evening of 20 July, the Navy gun crew had stood its general-quarters watch for one hour before and after sunset. After securing from our alert and setting normal watches, I went to dinner in the officers' wardroom, where the mates and engineers who were off watch were still discussing "that ship."

Except that the wind out of the southwest had started to freshen, 21 July was an uneventful day. Then, during the 4 to 8 evening watch, while the gun crew was at general quarters, a Navy seaman on lookout in the forward-gun tub reported sighting a sailing vessel on a southerly course about one mile off our starboard bow. A sailing vessel? On the high seas? In wartime 1944?

The report created excitement among all hands then on deck and gradually spread throughout the ship. Every crew member free to do so began to crowd the starboard rail to try to get a glimpse of the sailing ship. Few had ever seen a seagoing vessel under sail before.

And, sure enough, it was out there — a two- or three-masted sailing ship — its large sails barely visible in the twilight, tacking into the wind at five or six knots. Because of the distance and poor visibility, it was not possible to see flags or other identification, although the ship was assumed to be a neutral, probably Spanish or Argentine. This was confirmed as we passed the "sailor" abeam, when it was noted that the vessel had turned on a small display of lights on its main mast.

At sunset, we on *William Gaston* had the unusual wartime experience of having *two* neutral vessels reasonably close abeam — the Argentine freighter, northbound, a half mile off our starboard quarter, and an unidentified sailing ship, southbound, about one mile off our starboard beam. Both were showing running lights while we were blacked out.

At the time, the sailing ship incident seemed of little consequence, except to illustrate that, in a long wartime sea voyage, any unusual development, even the sighting of whales or porpoises, created excitement aboard ship. In this case, however, based on research done nearly 40 years later, it is now known that the Nazis used "neutral" sailing vessels as well as U-boats in carrying on their clandestine operations in Argentina.

At midnight on 20 July, I again listened to the BBC news from London in the radio shack with Operator Lester Godown. I then turned in for the night feeling pretty good about my recent experiences in Uruguay and Argentina, and happy to be heading back to the U.S.A.

Chapter 11

Sunday,
23 July 1944

The calendar of that date indicated that the day was Sunday, but on a Merchant ship at sea during the war, one day of the week was like any other. There were no church services, no Sunday papers, no days off, no family dinners, no Sunday evening radio programs — none of the traditions which made Sunday a special day for people back home.

At daybreak, *William Gaston* was about 1,000 miles out of Buenos Aires, but no longer heading for Rio de Janeiro. On the previous day, our ship had received a direct radio message, in code, from USN Com Fourth Fleet, ordering the ship to make an abrupt change of course from 025° to 090°, or from northeasterly to eastward. A direct message to a specific Merchant ship was, in itself, very unusual in wartime communications.

It was my responsibility to decode the message, and when I handed it to Captain Chase, he read it in disbelief and aggravation. He said something like, "That stupid U.S. Navy. First they order us to Rio — now they're sending us to Africa!"

It *was* an unusual and unexpected change of orders. But, at the time, we on *William Gaston* didn't attach too much significance to it. We were not aware then that the U.S. Navy was trying to route us around a new danger zone, following the torpedoing of a Brazilian ship on 20 July. As I recall, the reaction of most of our crew was simply one of disappointment that we would be later in reaching Rio and later in arriving back in the States.

Our only apparent problem that morning was the weather, which on 21-22 July had begun to produce heavy seas. I didn't understand it at the time, but now I know that there is a cold, gale-force wind which periodically blows in winter months from the south and west across the pampas of Argentina and is known as "the *Pampero*." As with other low barometric pressure storms, there were low-hanging clouds and rain squalls, and the high winds created enormous swells in the sea. The air was very cold but above freezing.

The 7,000-ton *William Gaston*, with its 9,000-ton cargo, was holding its own in the heavy seas, but the 200-ton Argentinian, still in pursuit, was being tossed about like a rubber duck.

During previous days, the unidentified Argentine ship had continued to track us, day and night, on our starboard quarter. We still didn't take it too seriously. As I remember, we began to agree with Captain Chase's opinion that the jerks didn't know how to navigate and were simply following us to Rio. They were so stupid that they didn't even realize that they were now following us toward Africa!

In the previous week, the dog Juan-Wan had become a pet of virtually the entire crew, and in a sense, everyone became a member of the conspiracy to conceal the dog's presence from Captain Chase. Although individual members had previously served at sea from a minimum of several months to a maximum of many years, none apparently had ever sailed before with a pet dog on board. In the human loneliness of life on an all-male ship, it was inevitable that a friendly dog would make friends among the crew, many of whom would save food from their meals in order to feed Juan-Wan. The dog's ultimate fate was a concern of many.

Then during the afternoon of Sunday, 23 July, an unusual event occurred, which could have been a fantasy directly out of "The Rime of the Ancient Mariner" by Samuel Taylor Coleridge. At about 3 p.m., a very large sea bird, later identified as an albatross, began circling the ship and giving out a kind of shrieking, crying call. The entire crew of the ship was attracted out on deck to watch this unusual spectacle.

Almost inconceivably, the bird suddenly dropped down and made a kind of crash landing on the deck, where it lay in a tangled heap as if it were exhausted, injured or ill, and perhaps dying. Bear in mind that a web-footed sea bird would never, under normal circumstances, try to make a landing on a solid surface like a steel deck.

As the bird lay prone and panting, the crew gathered closer to watch. Some of the older hands in the Merchant crew began to recall the traditional superstitions of mariners about the albatross. A live albatross brings good luck, a dead albatross brings disaster, they said.

During all this excitement, the "stowaway" dog Juan-Wan escaped from the Hobb-Sung stateroom, where he had been spending Sunday, which even at sea was a day of rest for some members of the Merchant crew. The dog ran out onto the main deck and started barking at the big strange bird.

Standing aloft on the starboard wing of the bridge, Captain Chase had been watching the drama of the fallen albatross and then suddenly became aware that he had an illegal animal on board. Momentarily, he had thoughts as to whom in the crew was responsible, and what problems might arise with health authorities when the ship reached Rio de Janeiro or, later, a U.S. port.

In order to resolve the problem, at least temporarily, Bosun Hobbs stepped forward, picked up the dog, and carried it aft to the paint locker, where he put it into its own sea-borne "dog house."

After about an hour resting and flopping on the deck, the big bird seemed to regain some of its strength and attempted to stand up or sit on its legs, but these were too weak to support its weight. Reference books I checked later describe the albatross, which lives only in the southern oceans, as having a wing span of 12 feet or more. However, my recollection of our guest on *William Gaston* is that it had a wing span of only 6 to 8 feet.

After a time it became apparent that the albatross was the victim of its own peculiar aerodynamics. With its large body, webbed feet, and weak legs, it simply could not take off from a steel deck. Finally, two Merchant seamen, wearing heavy gloves, volunteered to lift the squawking bird by its wings to the starboard rail and dropped it over the side. The entire crew gathered in the after sections of the ship to watch the albatross, again in its natural environment, riding up and down the high waves in the wake of the ship. Interestingly, in September 1834, while serving on the American brig *Pilgrim*, Richard Henry Dana, author of *Two Years Before the Mast*, recorded in his diary that *Pilgrim* had encountered a severe *Pampero* storm while sailing southward off the coast of Argentina and later saw albatrosses both in flight and on the rolling South Atlantic. Nature at sea doesn't change much from century to century.

At sunset our Navy Gun Crew stood its usual general quarters-watch, although this was conducted from upper-deck positions because heavy seas were breaking over the main deck on the starboard side. In fact, on Captain Chase's orders, all starboard doors on the main deck had been closed and "dogged" in order to keep the running seas from breaking into the midship house.

And then, almost eerily, we noticed that the mystery ship on our starboard quarter had also dropped back out of sight and disappeared.

As I recall, we all felt especially exhilarated at evening mess. The twin dramas of the albatross and the small Argentine ship had apparently ended agreeably, and we all looked forward to a good dinner and a good night's sleep.

After setting Navy watches for the night, I went to the officer's wardroom and joined the others for evening mess. As I recall, it was an excellent meal as even at sea the cooks tried to make Sunday dinners something special.

Now that Captain Chase was aware that Juan-Wan was on board, the dog was granted freedom to roam the main deck, including the crews' quarters and the mess halls. Needless to say, Juan-Wan attracted even more attention and affection than before.

After dinner I went to visit Chief Engineer Seaberg in his quarters on the boat deck around the passageway from my own stateroom. We talked about the albatross and the disappearance of the Argentinian ship. Although Chief Engineer Seaberg had sailed the seas for many years, mostly in the Northern Hemisphere, he had never before seen an albatross. As to the Argentinians, he believed that they had become aware that they were being led off course and had decided to try to find Rio on their own.

After 8 p.m., we were joined by First Engineer Walter Miller, who had just come off the 4 to 8 watch. We were reminiscing about our recent experiences in Buenos Aires and looking forward to Rio de Janeiro. For almost the first time we all felt very secure from U-boats because we *knew* the heavy seas would make it impossible for them to operate on or near the surface.

The time was about 8:27 p.m. . . .

Chapter 12

Disaster Strikes

Suddenly and without warning, at about 8:30 p.m., a tremendous explosion rocked *William Gaston*. The ship shuddered and all lights went out. Crew members ran into darkened passageways and shouted, "What was that? What was that?"

Second Mate Pennino, on watch in the wheel house, pushed the button for the general alarm to awaken sleeping members of the crew. Loud electrical bells rang throughout the midship house, adding the horror of their shrill sound to the terror of deathly darkness.

I groped my way around the corner of the passageway to my quarters and found my life jacket in the darkness. In leaving the stateroom, I hesitated momentarily to consider whether there was anything else I wanted. Under the circumstances, material possessions seemed very unimportant. I wasn't even adequately clothed. I was wearing a khaki shirt and trousers, and I was shoeless in stockinged feet.

I remembered that there were battery-powered portable emergency lights mounted on the bulkheads in the passageway, but because I had never tried to remove one before, I was frustrated and near panic before I found that it was necessary to rotate the lamp one-quarter turn in order to lift it out of its bulkhead bracket.

Meanwhile, crewmen on the lower main deck were temporarily trapped as the outer doors there were closed and "dogged" because of the heavy seas. Finally, they scrambled up the ladders to the inside of the boat deck, where, in the darkness, they bounced against each other and the bulkheads.

With the emergency light, I was able to find my way to the flying bridge — the top of the midship house, which was my emergency battle station. I found that the Navy's sound-powered telephones were still operative and that the

The sinking of the *William Gaston*. The original oil painting, "Death of a Liberty Ship," by American marine artist Herb Hewitt of Wakefield, Massachusetts. The survivors are on the raft in the foreground; the life ring with emergency light is near the raft.

Navy crews were at their stations at guns on the bow and stern. However, we could see nothing in the darkness, made worse by blinding salt spray from the wind-swept crests of waves.

Any sort of defense seemed out of the question. At first we weren't even sure what had happened, until Navy Gunner's Mate Walter Lang, in charge of the stern-gun crew, told me by phone that one of the Navy seamen on watch reported that we had been torpedoed on the starboard side aft.

I then remember going down one level to the bridge deck and reporting that to Captain Chase. It was his responsibility to judge the condition of the ship and to give the order to abandon if he considered that necessary or advisable. At the same time, the engine room gang was already milling around the boat deck with the rest of the crew. The ship was losing headway in the water and seemed to be sinking slowly by the stern. Accordingly, at about 8:34 p.m., the captain passed the word to "Abandon Ship." I shouted that word by phone to the gun crews on the bow and stern. We were about to try to abandon in very heavy seas.

The first boat to be lowered was the Captain's Boat, #1 forward on the starboard side. Because that was the weather side, it was impossible from the outset. Several crewmen climbed into the boat. The davits were swung out over the side, and the falls were partially lowered. But as the boat reached the ship's freeboard, the heavy seas picked it up and banged it into the side of the ship. Within a minute or so, it became apparent that no lifeboat could possibly be launched into such seas. As a result, it then became necessary to rescue the seamen who were already in the boat. This was finally achieved by forming a "human chain" and pulling the men back on board before the seas broke up the lifeboat.

In the melee, I had momentary eye-to-eye contact with Gunner's Mate Lang. His face was in a kind of shock, his eyes open but apparently unseeing. He was an experienced Navy man. He was no more frightened than the rest of us. I just remember *his* face over 40 years later.

In the confusion, I again found Captain Chase, and we agreed (it was *his* responsibility) that we should douse the lights and hope that the ship would somehow stay afloat until morning. I passed the word to the Navy crew to take positions as high in the ship as possible, where they would be safer from another torpedo.

Then, simply because I was trying to calm my nerves by *doing something constructive*, I shouted to Captain Chase, "Captain, we should throw the Navy code books overboard!"

He agreed, shouting back, "Do it!"

I ran up the ladder to his stateroom, where the codes were kept in a perforated steel case. I carried the case out to the starboard wing of the bridge. Then, before dropping it over the side, I had a second thought. *Suppose we don't sink after all?*

I put the steel case down on the exposed deck and started looking aft on the starboard side. By this time, with the lights out, my night vision was restored, and I could see the after-half of the ship fairly clearly as she was being pounded by steady heavy seas over the starboard rail. I remember thinking with numbed emotions that it would be a long night before daybreak.

The time was about 8:38 p.m. . . . .

While standing on the starboard wing of the bridge looking aft, I had a full view of the explosion of a second torpedo, again on the starboard quarter at about #4 hold. Hatch covers blew into the air and overhead booms began to crash to the deck. The most memorable aspect was the sickening smell of the explosive charge, which was carried forward by the southwest wind.

After that there were no more orders and no communications of any kind — just 67 unorganized men trying to escape a now-certain sinking ship by whatever means were available. Lifeboat #1 on the starboard side had already been lost, and #3 seemed to face a similar fate in the same heavy seas. Boats #2 and 4 on the port side were somewhat in the lee of the weather and had a chance to be successfully lowered, as their assigned crews had been standing by them during our temporary blackout.

Having lost #1 boat, and with # 2, 3, and 4 taken, there were still 14 Navy and Merchant crewmen on the boat deck with no boat available. In the midst of the confusion, First Engineer Walter Miller noted that, under my life jacket, I was wearing only a khaki shirt and trousers. He went back into his nearby stateroom and brought me his trench coat. Although I eventually lost the coat while abandoning ship, I still remember his thoughtfulness as perhaps one of the most compassionate acts ever extended to me.

With all the boats gone and the ship sinking rapidly by the stern, those of us on the port-side boat deck were now in a very precarious situation. And then our "prisoner," Navy Seaman Walter Smith, whom we had picked up in Santos, rose to the occasion. He scrambled down a ladder to the main deck and was able to release a large life raft from its slide mount on the forward port side. The raft hit water and was held alongside by a heavy rope line called a "painter," which kept lifeboats and life rafts from drifting astern of a ship still underway.

With our emergency lamps, which were now back in use, we scrambled pell-mell down the ladder to the main deck, and literally *walked up the deck* of the stern-sinking ship to the point where the raft was alongside just below the rail. We actually jumped over the side and onto the raft. As I recall, I was the second to the last man to leave the ship — nothing heroic, just not eager to give up a large ship for a small raft. The last man to abandon, as I definitely recall, was the Radio Operator, Norman Lester Godown, who had remained at his post in the radio shack, not just until the last minute but literally until the *final seconds.*

With the ship now in an almost upright position and sinking rapidly by the stern, the crew on the raft was still attached to the ship by the heavy painter. Again, Navy Seaman Smith rose to the occasion by cutting the thick line with his *demand knife!* We were now free of the ship, but dangerously close aboard.

The second torpedo apparently had damaged the ship's steam lines in such a way that the steam whistle on the stack had started blowing continuously, again adding terrifying sound to the scene of disaster. The ship was like a giant sea beast screaming in its death throes.

Everything loose on deck was tumbling aft toward the sinking stern. Seawater was pouring into open hatches, replacing air which roared to the surface.

We on the raft were afloat but immobilized under the port bow. There were oars lashed to the raft but no possible way to use them. With our emergency lights, we could see that we were dangerously under the huge anchor hanging from the port hawsehole.

And then, as our flashlights panned across the rapidly sinking ship, we saw one brief heart-rending sight, which seemed even more obscene than the horrifying event itself. On the boat deck of *William Gaston* stood the dog Juan-Wan, barking at us between the rails, unable to make himself heard over the din of other horrifying noises.

As the groaning ship went down violently, the anchor narrowly missed the raft. There was no evidence of the anticipated downward suction. In fact, the sinking actually created a swell which seemed to push the raft away from the vortex.

The final moments were beyond description. Seawater poured down the open gangways of the ship, struck the hot boiler, and set off a series of enormous underwater eruptions. Almost mercifully, the damnable steam whistle was drowned into silence. The ship had sunk in three minutes after the second torpedo.

During the first few minutes on the raft, we all must have been in a state of semi-shock and became seasick. Almost simultaneously, every man became nauseous and vomited all over himself and the others. The raft, as I recall, measured about 9 feet by 12 feet by 3 feet deep. It was constructed of heavy lattice-like wooden timbers, which held eight or ten steel drums that provided bouyancy.

As the raft rode up and down between the troughs and crests of the waves, sometimes half turning on the slopes, we could do nothing but just hang on as the seas repeatedly crashed over the raft, first from one side and then another. With no visible horizon between sea and sky, with no sense of direction of up and down, and with plankton in the water producing flashes of irridescent light, it was like a combination roller-coaster flume ride suspended in cosmic space.

During the first hour we saw several star shells rise and fall in the darkened sky. At first we wishfully thought that these were signs of rescue efforts, but we soon realized that they had been fired by our friends in the lifeboats. At one point during the night the Radio Operator, who as noted was on the raft, told us that he had sent repeated SOS messages but had received no acknowledgement. We were then hanging onto a raft in a very rough sea nearly 200 miles off the coast of southern Brazil — far outside of coastal shipping lanes and with little or no trans-Atlantic traffic in that latitude. Our prospects were not very promising.

It was then about 9:30 p.m. I remember thinking *again* that it would be a long night before daylight.

During the night the men on the raft could do nothing but try to hold on tightly to their small floating island, which was only a few inches above sea level. Each kept his private thoughts or prayers. No one spoke. It was a *very* long night.

Chapter 13

A Miracle Occurs

From the sea-level viewpoint of a large, crowded life raft floating on a rolling sea, sunrise in the South Atlantic on 24 July 1944 literally defied description. After long hours of an eerie blue and black nighttime phantasmagoria, the eastern sky began to turn purple and then red as the rising sun, still below the horizon, began to illuminate the low hanging storm clouds. These, in turn, reflected roseate light down onto the sea and converted it into a kaleidoscope of changing colors.

Meanwhile, although the wind had abated somewhat, the sea was still rolling heavily, and the raft continued to ride up from the troughs to the crests and back down again. Ironically, in the early morning light, the view was as much like rolling sand dunes in the Sahara as of rolling seas in the South Atlantic.

After dawn had finally broken and a new day had begun, we began to take stock of our situation. We opened a trap door in the middle of the raft to check our survival equipment. What we found was not very reassuring. First of all, there was a wooden keg for fresh water, which, it turned out, had apparently never been checked since the ship was launched in 1942. The steel band at one end of the keg had slipped off, the wooden base was gone, and our fresh water supply consisted of a mere shell of a keg, floating in seawater.

There was also a small steel cylinder designed to hold emergency food rations, but this produced only hard chocolate which, upon inspection, was found to be full of white worms. We eventually ate small pieces of the chocolate, but only after carefully removing the worms.

Ironically, the men responsible for such gross neglect of maintenance — several members of the deck crew — were with us on the raft. Others no doubt were undergoing similar experiences in the lifeboats. However, perhaps strangely, there were no recriminations among passengers on the raft. We were only interested in hoping to survive.

Meanwhile, we had no choice except to hang on and wait for what we could not even guess. The ship's lifeboats had disappeared completely, and we felt very alone on an enormous sea. The South Atlantic winter air was very cold but bearable. Our latitude was 30° South, roughly comparable to that of Jacksonville, Florida, which is about 30° North.

During the morning, because of rolling seas, crowding and exhaustion, a number of men on the raft slipped over the side and had to be pulled back aboard again. Some of us were concerned about sharks, but these were never a threat. However, we were discovered and followed by curious sea gulls, which could have been knocked down, taken, and eaten in a serious emergency. This gave us a new insight into the survival of Captain Eddie Rickenbacker of the U.S. Army Air Forces, who, along with crew mates, had survived a long ordeal in a lifeboat in the Pacific by subsisting on the raw flesh of captured sea gulls.

* * *

In retrospect, the men on our raft were a rather interesting heterogeneous group, brought together entirely by chance. There were, as I recall, about equal numbers of the Merchant and Navy crews, and we got along excellently together. The senior "passenger" was Chief Mate Chalk, the former British Merchant Master. Also aboard were First Engineer Miller and Radio Operator Godown, both of whom I still remember as great guys. Among the Merchant and Navy crewmen there was also Navy Seaman Walter Smith, whose knife had made it possible for all of us to be floating on a raft in the South Atlantic on 24 July 1944.

During the morning, as I recall, we all gradually became rather depressed about our propsects. Our plight was presumably unknown to U.S. Naval authorities. We were far outside normal coastal shipping lanes. We had no water to drink and no food except wormy chocolate. One minor point may be worth mentioning. After we all were nauseous during the previous night, none of us had need to urinate again while we were on the raft. I do not presume to understand that phenomenon, but I have a feeling that there may be some kind of automatic mechanism in nature which may help a stricken animal without water from becoming dehydrated. Just a thought.

At about mid-morning, several of the survivors on the outer edges of the raft reported that the craft seemed to be slowly losing freeboard and gradually sinking down to the level of the sea. Chief Mate Chalk, the most experienced sailor on board, said he thought one or more of the steel drums must have been taking in sea water and the raft was probably losing its buoyancy. Not a very encouraging development under the circumstances.

As the hours dragged on slowly, we spent the time just trying to hang on to the raft, riding up and down on still mountainous waves. At noon the sun was high over head, but that was about the only normal condition in a now strange world. Gradually all conversation ceased, and we drifted into a mood of silent despair.

At about 1 p.m., a *miracle* occurred for the benefit of the 14 men on the life raft. Suddenly, someone shouted "Look, look, an airplane!" We all looked in the indicated direction, and, sure enough there *was* an aircraft in the distance. In the initial excitement, there was an immediate fear that the plane would not see us and simply fly away. Several men stood up on the crowded raft, waving their arms and shouting futilely.

But the aircraft *did* see us and began to fly a wide circle, gradually dropping to a lower altitude. After a few minutes the plane passed directly over the raft. We could see from its markings that it was a U.S. Navy seaplane of the Mariner class (PBM). As it passed over, the co-pilot on the right-hand side of the cockpit flashed the "V for Victory" sign in Morse code with a hand-held blinker light.

For the benefit of younger readers, it may be useful to point out here that "V for Victory" had become a rallying symbol for Allied Forces. The Morse code sign for the letter "V" — three dots and a dash — could be shown by an upraised hand with the first and second fingers forming a "V" or it could be transmitted by sound signal or blinker light. Ironically, it became associated with the opening bars of the German composer Beethoven's Fifth Symphony — "da, da, da, dah."

Naturally, a tremendous feeling of excitement and exhiliration swept through the raft's crew. We didn't know how or when or even if we would be rescued, but we were greatly reassured by the knowledge that Naval authorities somewhere would soon learn of our plight.

During the ensuing afternoon, the raft was kept under surveillance almost continuously by one or more Mariners on a series of patrols. The weather had abated somewhat, but the seas seemed still far too rough for seaplane landings. We had no ideas about a rescue plan or *how* or *from where* it might be conducted. Nevertheless, we were enormously reassured that the planes were keeping a constant eye on us. As I recall, we thought that perhaps they were trying to keep our morale up. But we later learned that there was a far more practical purpose. The raft was drifting farther and farther to sea, and the Squadron Commander did not wish to lose contact and have to start the search all over again.

We also learned later there was hope that weather conditions might moderate sufficiently to permit landings on the ocean and achieve rescue of the survivors by seaplanes. However, that hope did not materialize.

Above: A U.S. Navy Mariner seaplane 201-P-1, similar to the one piloted by Lieutenant (jg) Charles E. Snyder, USNR, which discovered the survivors of the *William Gaston* while on routine anti-submarine patrol in the South Atlantic.

Below: The U.S. Navy seaplane tender USS *Matagorda*, which picked up the survivors of the *William Gaston* and put them ashore in Florianopolis, Brazil. (Photos, U.S. Navy, courtesy of National Archives)

As the sun began to sink on the western horizon, we on the raft witnessed another breathtaking scene in our strange world between the sea and the sky. It was like a slow-motion color movie of that morning's sunrise, but with the film *run backwards*. The whites, blues, and grays of the day began to change to shades of red, then deep purple, then black. We had no choice except to try to hang on as our craft began its second night on our roller-coaster flume ride.

With another 12 hours of darkness in prospect, we again became somewhat depressed, having then gone more than 24 hours without sleep, food, or water, and with no sign of rescue yet in sight.

During the night we were surprised and reassured that the PBMs continued to try to keep us under surveillance. This they did by turning on their landing lights and trying to spot us on the vast dark sea. It was an eerie sensation to hear and see a huge roaring plane repeatedly fly past on the beam of the raft, first on one side and then on another. Finally, one of the pilots tried a different method, which worked. By turning off his landing lights and flying at a very low altitude, he found he could see clusters of small red emergency lights, which were attached to the life jackets of all survivors.

Finally, at about 3 a.m., we were startled to see a huge searchlight at some distance on the surface, scanning the sea in obvious search for something. Was it a U-boat or a friendly vessel? We really didn't know.

After a few minutes, the beam located the raft and blinded us in its glare. The vessel moved closer until it reached a distance of perhaps a hundred yards. Then a voice with an amplifier sang out, "Ahoy there. Stand by to take a line."

A small gun boomed on deck, and the projectile carrying the line fell short. A second shot went wide. Then, to our consternation, the ship started up its engines, doused the light, and moved off into the distance. Later, we learned that the Commander of the rescue vessel, with a load of aviation gasoline and anti-submarine bombs on board, sensibly did not wish to risk his ship to U-boats by lying dead in the water for an extended period.

In about 30 minutes, the ship again approached the raft, found us with its light, and fired another line. This time the distance and direction were accurate. Several men made the line fast to the raft, and using its deck winch, the ship pulled us alongside to a gangway which had been lowered on the lee side.

Although we had suffered no great physical hardships, the men on the raft were emotionally spent, tired, and weak from lack of water, sleep, and exercise, and had to be half-carried up the gangway of USS *Matagorda*, a Navy seaplane tender. We were given, as I recall, water and a bowl of soup and crewmen's bunks for much-needed rest. Meanwhile, the raft had been sunk by machine-gun fire.

During the next few hours of fitful sleep, I was repeatedly awakened by the Officer of the Watch, who wanted to know how many lifeboats there were and

CONFIDENTIAL

NAVY DEPARTMENT
OFFICE OF THE CHIEF OF NAVAL OPERATIONS
WASHINGTON 25, D. C.

Op-16-B-5

21 August 1944

MEMORANDUM FOR FILE

ALL TIMES GCT

SUBJECT: Summary of Statements by Survivors of the SS WILLIAM GASTON, American Freighter, 7177 G.T., owned by War Shipping Administration, operated by American West African Lines, Inc.

1.   The WILLIAM GASTON was torpedoed at 0130 GCT, 24 July 1944, in 26.37 S - 46.13 W, having sailed from Buenos Aires, 19 July, independently for Baltimore, Maryland, with 9038 tons of corn. Vessel sank stern first at approximately 0143.
2.   Ship was on an unknown course, speed 10.1 knots, not zigzagging, blacked out. The weather was cloudy, with occasional squalls and rain, sea heavy, wind SW force 5-6, no ships in sight.
3.   At 0130 a torpedo struck on the starboard side between #4 and #5 holds approximately 10' below the waterline. Explosion gave off a muffled sound. Third mate on bridge saw fire shoot out toward the port quarter although ship was hit on starboard. No. 5 hatch blew open, hatch beams were on port deck, and end of port #5 boom was in the water. Maize was all over the deck. Steam was blowing off and engines secured immediately. All lights went out. Distress signals were sent but it is not known whether they got on the air or not. At approximately 0140 a second torpedo struck on the starboard side about 20' forward of the sternpost. Explosion was twice as loud as the first, gave off a flash and a heavy black smoke. Ship turned over to port and sank stern first with no suction at about 0143. No counter offensive possible. Confidential codes were thrown overboard.
4.   Ship was in the process of being abandoned when second torpedo struck. No. 1 lifeboat was lowered and destroyed by heavy sea; #2, #3, #4 boats and 1 raft were successfully launched. At 1200, 24 July, survivors sighted a plane. At 1300 a message was received by the USS MATAGORDA from Searching Plane #8 of Squadron 203, reporting 3 boat loads of survivors and a large amount of floating debris nearby, position 26.32S - 46.15W bearing 068° true from Avoredo Island Light, distance 124 miles. The MATAGORDA proceeded to area and the first boat was sighted in 26.03 S - 46.24W, and survivors removed at 0631, 25 July. A total of 3 boats and 1 raft were located and all personnel removed. At 1005 ship set course for Florianopolis and arrived at 1900. Total complement on board was 67, including 41 crew and 26 Armed Guard; all 67 survived.
5.   The sub was not sighted. The radio operator stated that while he was on the bridge just after the first torpedo struck, the Captain and he saw a small winking light about one or two points abaft the starboard beam and apparently about 1/4 mile or less away which may have been the sub that torpedoed the ship.

BARBARA CONARD,
Lt. (jg) W-V(S), USNR.

DISSEMINATION: Op-16-E-2, 16-P-1, 16-Z(5 copies), Op-20-G-M, Op-23-L, Op-30-M, Op-39-P-3(2 copies), COMINCH F-20, F-21, F-41, FX-37 (C&R), FX-43, FX-45, AFASU, BuOrd, BuShips, CG(4 copies), Coord Res & Dev, JAG, DIO 1,3,4,5(2 copies), 6, 7(3 copies), 8(2 copies), 10(4 copies), 11(3 copies), 12, 13, 14(4 copies), 15 NDs, Op-28, BuOrd (Re-6-a), BuPers 535.

CONFIDENTIAL

CONFIDENTIAL   CONFIDENTIAL   CONFIDENTIAL

how many crewmen had been aboard *William Gaston*. I was unsure how many lifeboats had gotten away, but I knew there were 27 members of the Navy gun crew, and I thought about 40 Merchant officers and men.

During the last hours of darkness, while I finally slept, *Matagorda* picked up crew from three lifeboats, one carrying Captain Chase, and then sank the

Survivors of SS *William Gaston*

Merchant Officers and Crew
Captain Harry W. CHASE
First Mate Ernest CHALK (British)
Second Mate James Victor PENNINO
Third Mate Howard CARANDEE ˙
Radio Operator Forman Lester GODOWN
Purser Marshall Edward MAXWELL
Bos'n Alonsa A. HOBBS
Carpenter Ivan EHMAN

Able-bodied Seamen
Henry McMILLAN
Peter A. ELSESSER
Jaime VIOR (Spanish)
Mathew PRIBITNOWSKI
Beecher J. HIGBY
Thomas NOBLE

Ordinary Seamen
Frank MENDYKE
Joseph BODNAR
Victor PEREZ (Spanish)

Steward Department
Steward Canute McKAY
Chief Cook Chow SUNG (Chinese)
Second Cook John STEWART (Honduran)
Third Cook Stanley H. WHIRLEY

Engineering Department
Chief Engineer Gustav SEABERG
First Ass't. Engineer Walter F. MILLER
Second Ass't. Engineer John V. FARRAR
Third Ass't. Engineer John O. MEE
Jr. Engineer Francis BAUSER
Deck Engineer Michael P. McLAUGHLIN (Irish)

Oilers
James O. DOWNEY
Sidney Richard DAVIS
William Adam BENDER

Firemen
Louis LAURENT
Clair V. WALSH
Ramon BILBAO (Spanish)

Wipers
Percy M. SCHMEHL
James B. PAUL

Messmen	**Utility Men**
Harold WARREN	James Nelson DAVIS
Octavian T. PAPES	Adam Edward BROWN
John Henry BAILEY	Bernard Harland FOLLETT

U.S. Navy Armed Guard Gun Crew
Lieutenant (jg) Harold Joseph McCORMICK, 243934, D-V(S), USNR
MARTIN, Sot, Jr., 829 05 68, Slc., USNR
SALSGENER, Reginald Dennis, 313 01 87, Slc., USNR
REICHMANN, Kirbey Joseph, 272 84 52, SM2c., USN
BIDDLE, Edwin MacFunn, III, 246 24 95, Slc., USNR
SMITH, Walter, 856 36 96, Slc., USN
REEVES, Samuel Norman, 856 60 RS, GR3c., USN
FLEMMING, Gerald LeRoy, 856 75 64, Slc., USNR
DENNING, Carlton B., 828 90 48, SLC., USNR
PATTERSON, George William, 658 38 49, Cox, USNR
BOHANAN, Frank James, 832 65 37, Slc., USNR
MULVIHILL, John William, 857 63 42m, Slc., USNR
PAPPAS, John Joseph, 906 42 45m, Slc., USNR
LANG, Walter James, 612 51 10, GM3c., USNR
BURKE, Raymond Leon, 828 00 78, Slc., USNR
HOUSTON, Ralph Linwood, 208 86 90, Slc., USNR
LAVERTY, Franklyn Norman, 906 87 84, Slc., USNR
MASAROVICH, Charles, 816 92 17, Slc., USN
SHEARIN, Frank Jr., 863 82 89, Slc., USN
GUSTINA, John Edward, 609 46 35m, Slc., USNR
SUMMERS, James John, 820 28 62, Slc., USNR
JONETT, Joseph William, 306 29 76, Slc., USNR
WILLIAMS, Bernard, 843 62 41, Slc., USNR
BENOIT, Eugene, 644 64 46, GM3c., USNR
CRANFORD, Dick Ross, 829 84 11, Slc., USNR
FARMER, Donald Gene, 569 06 76, Slc., USNR

Source: Report by Commander Andrew A. Crinkley, USN, of USS *Matagorda*. (Courtesy of National Archives)

boats by machine-gun fire. Boat #1, which was never launched, eventually washed up on a beach in southern Brazil.

After we had had a few hours' sleep and a new day had dawned, the survivors of *William Gaston* began to gather in *Matagorda's* messhalls — the Merchant officers and myself in the officers' wardroom, the Navy enlisted men and ship's crew in the enlisted men's mess.

Our principal reaction was simply one of just being happy to be alive and grateful to our rescuers. The ship's mess served us what Navy ships always considered a "big spread" for breakfast — crisp bacon, scrambled powdered eggs, toast, butter, and gallons of black coffee. However, the survivors really did not have appetites equal to the hospitality.

In the officers' wardroom, Captain Chase, Chief Mate Chalk, Chief Engineer Seaberg, myself, and the other Merchant officers sat over coffee with *Matagorda* Commander Andrew A. Crinkley, USN, and several of his officers. There was so much to say, but so little that could be said.

In the course of conversation, it turned out that both of our Chiefs, Chalk and Seaberg, had been in the British Merchant Marine during World War I and both had survived torpedoings by German U-boats. Both Commander Crinkley and Captain Chase had served in the U.S. Navy during that war. Gradually, I found myself thinking, *what's a greenhorn landlubber from Indiana like me doing with a group like this?*

The *Matagorda* was headed at flank speed on a westerly course toward Florianopolis, Brazil, its current temporary base. There was a notable nervousness among the officers due to the ship's present predicament. Although it was *Matagorda's* mission to seek out and destroy U-boats, without her Mariners she had no means to attack submarines or even protect herself from their possible attack.

We survivors of *William Gaston* literally had nothing in our possession except the clothes on our backs — no money, no identification, and, in some cases, no shoes. The crew of *Matagorda* was as helpful as possible, but there were practical limitations as to what assistance they could offer. Besides, with 67 extra "passengers" on board, the ship was very crowded — in the mess halls, in the sleeping quarters, and especially in the heads.

During the afternoon, Commander Crinkley received a dispatch from USN Com Fourth Fleet, instructing him to land the survivors at Florianopolis and to turn them over to the custody of the U.S. Vice Consul stationed there.

After a long and nervous day, *Matagorda* reached the safety of San Miguel Bay early in the evening of 25 July. In the twilight we could see four Mariners riding at anchor on the bay, their crews still aboard. Without the seaplane tender, and with no base ashore, the men were without facilities for either eating or sleeping.

Soon after dropping anchor, *Matagorda* lowered a gig to pick up the aircraft crews and bring them aboard the tender. Over dinner, the officers and men of *William Gaston* had an opportunity to meet and thank the PBM crews, who had found us and watched over us throughout a long day and night.

We were especially pleased to meet Lieutenant Charles Snyder, USNR, the pilot and captain of Mariner #203-P-8, and to hear from him his own story of first sighting a floating smoke pot, thinking it was a U-boat's snorkel, and starting a bombing run until he saw one of our lifeboats nearby!

At 12:55 p.m., 26 July, after a more relaxing night on *Matagorda*, a launch from Florianopolis was brought alongside the ship's lowered gangway, and the crew of *William Gaston* disembarked, with a "hip-hip-hooray . . . hip-hip-hooray . . . hip-hip-hooray" to the *Matagorda* crew.

Although the prospect of setting our feet on dry land again was very reassuring, we were then being put ashore in a strange place over 5,000 miles from our home port of New York City, and with no apparent way to get there. Besides, there were the small problems of having no shoes, inadequate clothing, and no funds to fulfill our basic needs.

Nevertheless, as the launch approached a small fishing dock on the waterfront of Florianopolis, we all were in good spirits. Whatever the future held in store for us, it was far better than our prospects of several days earlier.

U. S. S. Merchant Seamen's Club of Rio

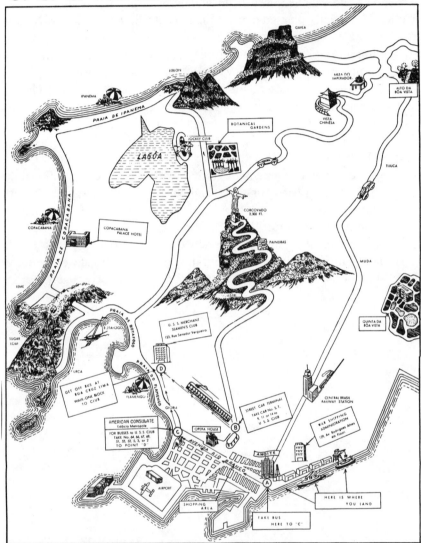

HOW TO REACH THE U. S. S. MERCHANT SEAMEN'S CLUB OF RIO DE JANEIRO

You land at "A" on the map. This is the Praça Mauá. If you land at one of the docks further down, take a streetcar to the Praça Mauá. Cross the Praça and take No. 1 bus (fare 20 centavos) to last stop. "C" on map. This is the Avenida Presidente Wilson, where the American Consulate and American Embassy are located.

At this point take any bus numbered 64, 52, 51, 53, 5, 3, 2, 68, 66, or 67. (Fare 60 centavos). Ride to point "D" on map. *Rua Cruz Lima* walk one block to right to U. S. S. **MERCHANT SEAMEN'S CLUB** at *Rua Senador Vergueira, 123.*

═══ **ALTERNATE ROUTE** ═══

Take bus No. 1 as above, but get off at 4th stop, in front of Avenida Hotel. Walk through arcade to the large square "Largo Carioca". Across the square to the left you will see the trolley (bonde) terminal. Take streetcar No. 5, 7, 9, 11 or 14. These trolleys pass the U. S. S. **MERCHANT SEAMEN'S CLUB.** Look for the sign, it will be on your left.

IT'S REALLY NOT AS INVOLVED AS IT SOUNDS ═ FIND THE WAY ONCE ═ YOU'LL BE GLAD YOU DID !

Chapter 14

Brazil to New York

Just after noon on 26 July, as we walked up the small gangway to the wooden pier extending out from the Florianopolis waterfront, we were greeted by a young man in his thirties who introduced himself by saying, "Hi, I'm Bill Rambo. I'm the U.S. Vice Consul here. Welcome to Florianopolis."

His full name, I later learned, was William Preston Rambo.

He was surrounded by a group of local Brazilian *officiales* who were shouting in Portuguese to each other and to others around the dock. Along the pier and up on shore were several hundred men, women, and children, also shouting and waving their arms. Obviously, the arrival of survivors from a torpedoed ship was a big event in wartime Florianopolis.

After introductions with the *Gaston* officers were completed, it became apparent that Mr. Rambo had been caught in the middle of a logistics problem for which he had neither staff nor facilities nor precedents to assist him. In retrospect, I have often empathized with the Vice Consul for the problem he faced that day. In the first place, there was the local transportation problem. There were no public vehicles available to transport 67 men for the mile or two from the harbor into the center of town. The survivors simply would have to walk, in a kind of ragtag parade formation.

Rambo had an American Jeep, which he drove himself. As I was the only U.S. Navy officer, he took the position that I was the "senior officer present" and offered me the other seat in his two-passenger car. That meant that I, as a young Junior-Grade Reserve Lieutenant, could ride, while the other survivors would have to walk, including Captain Chase and Chief Mate Chalk and Chief Engineer Seaberg, all of whom were by far my superiors both in age and in sea-going experience. In retrospect, I have often thought how they must have resented these arrangements.

Rambo drove slowly up the narrow road, leading the procession at the walkers' pace. The route was lined on both sides with townspeople waving and shouting. Rambo turned to me and said, "I think I should tell you that Florianopolis is primarily a German colony in Brazil. You can't be sure whether these people are cheering the survival of American seamen . . . or the success of German U-boats."

The Vice Consul's second problem had been in finding housing for his unexpected guests. Although there were several hotels in town, and not many visitors there during the war, Rambo had not had time to secure authorization from the Embassy in Rio de Janeiro or the State Department in Washington to make a financial commitment to hotel owners on the part of the U.S. government.

Under the circumstances, Rambo's housing arrangements for his 67 visitors now seem quite ingenious. Within the few hours' lead time before the survivors arrived, he had made arrangements with the local Brazilian army commander to house the U.S. Navy crew in a nearby military barracks. Because these facilities could not accommodate the full 67 extra men, Rambo then persuaded local civilian authorities to house *William Gaston's* Merchant officers and crew in the local jail! By this time, Captain Chase must have been totally outraged!

However, even under these conditions, a degree of poetic justice came into play on behalf of the Merchant officers and men.

After the Navy and Merchant crews had walked to their respective lodgings, Consul Rambo invited me to be his house guest at a comfortable, but not pretentious, private home in the hills overlooking the town and the harbor. He offered me a Scotch-and-soda, which was very welcome, and then instructed his Brazilian housekeeper to prepare a broiled dinner of locally caught fish.

Over dinner, Rambo told me that his home town in the U.S. was Hamilton, Ohio, not far from my own in Indiana, that he had joined the State Department before the war and had been sent to Brazil because he had majored in college in foreign languages, including Spanish and Portuguese.

After dinner we studied his *U.S. State Department Instruction Manual for Consular Personnel*, especially those sections dealing with the handling of "Stranded U.S. Seamen."

In the case of Merchant Marine personnel, a Consul's authority was clearly stated. He could give any stranded U.S. Merchant seaman the local equivalent of 100 U.S. dollars and could commit the U.S. government to pay for any available transportation to the nearest U.S. port.

However, in the case of U.S. Naval personnel, the instructions were very brief and set a kind of precedent for "Catch-22." The manual simply said: "Refer Navy personnel to the nearest U. S. Naval facility." That was located in Rio de Janeiro, nearly 1,000 miles to the north, and there was no transportation available — at least no service then operating under wartime conditions.

The following morning Rambo and I drove down to a local bank, where he withdrew some funds and gave them to me as a personal loan. I don't remember the amount, but it was sufficient for me to buy shoes, a change of khaki clothing, and to give some "beer money" to the Navy crewmen, who were already out seeing the limited sights of the town.

On 29 July, as a result of arrangements made by the U.S. Embassy in Rio de Janeiro, all Merchant and Navy survivors of *William Gaston* were placed aboard the Brazilian coastal steamer *Itabera* for passage to Rio. This was perhaps the most nerve-shaking phase of the whole experience — being on a slow, unescorted ship moving northward through the same waters in which we had been torpedoed less than a week earlier. *Itabera* was an old but well-appointed ship, which, in the tradition of passenger liners, served four meals a day. However, I had little appetite. I tried to sleep during the daytime and spent the nights walking the dim, blue-lighted passageways, carrying a life jacket.

On 1 August the ship put in for several hours at Santos, where Captain Chase and I went ashore for another visit with our friend, James Bacon, who was shocked to learn of the fate of *William Gaston*.

On 3 August *Itabera* entered and tied up in the beautiful harbor of Rio de Janeiro, where the Merchant crew was received by the U.S. Consul General, and Navy personnel were taken into the custody of U.S. Naval authorities. Thus, the Merchant and Navy crews were separated, and we never saw each other again.

For the Navy crew, Rio was very rewarding. We were provided with comfortable Navy quarters, we were given emergency pay allowances, we replaced parts of our lost uniforms, and we had free time to see the sights of Rio. From Navy Relief, I obtained funds to repay Vice Consul Rambo.

With several other Navy officers I had dinner one evening at Copacabana Palace Hotel and saw the most spectacular nightclub floor show I ever saw before or since. During the days I made the usual tourist excursions, including a visit to Mount Corcovado overlooking the broad Rio harbor, where the giant statue of Christ the Redeemer with arms outstretched stands. Because of its high elevation, that colossal work of art seems to dwarf our own Statue of Liberty.

On 7 August the Navy crew was provided transportation to the U.S. Naval Air Station to board a Naval Air Transport (NATS) DC-3 equipped with wartime "bucket seats," for a flight from Rio to Bahia and then to Recife, 1,200 miles up the coast. At the latter port, we were transferred to a Naval hospital which had been built in the jungle outside the city. We had no real need for hospitalization, but I sensed that the hospital and its staff *were* currently under-utilized! My principal recollection of the place is the fact that we could look out our windows and see wild monkeys playing in the trees.

Above: A Douglas DC-3 (U.S. Navy R4D) at an American military airstrip in 1944 in northern Brazil. Local workers are in the foreground.

Below: Fuel for the Naval Air Transport Service (NATS) aircraft was shipped in drums from the U.S. in American freighters to Brazilian seaports and then trucked over land to the airships. (Photos, U.S. Navy, courtesy of National Archives)

During our stay at the hospital, the Navy crew had many hours together to reminisce of its experiences since sailing from New York three months earlier. One of the stories which I still recall concerned a young Navy seaman from a well-known East Coast family. His shipmates said that "he was stewed, screwed, tattooed, and torpedoed on his first trip to sea!"

On 12 August the Navy crew was again placed aboard a NATS DC-3 for transportation to New York City. This eventually required six days because the plane could fly only during daylight and made long refueling or overnight stopovers at Natal, Fortaleza, and Belem in Brazil; Cayenne in French Guiana; Paramaribo in Dutch Guiana; Georgetown in British Guiana; Port of Spain in Trinidad; San Juan in Puerto Rico; Guantanamo in Cuba; and Miami, Florida, before the final leg to New York.

In those days there were no aircraft navigation aids at those primitive military airports in Latin America. For that reason, and because of the frequent landings, it was often necessary for the NATS planes to fly along a narrow corridor or shelf between the bottom of low-lying clouds along the coast and the tops of trees in the jungles. Those were really "white knuckle" flights. At each stop, the commander of the airstrip reviewed the priority of passengers and the number which safely could be carried on the heavily loaded aircraft, which also carried mail and cargo. Before each takeoff, the approved passengers were required to complete a rather unnerving "boarding pass," a form which simply requested name, rank or rate, and serial number, and *next of kin*!

After reaching New York alone on 19 August, I took a taxi to Brooklyn and reported in at the Armed Guard Center. It was still the hustling, bustling military establishment, with scores of officers and hundreds of enlisted men moving about in various stages of routine processing.

When I was about to report to the Duty Officer that morning, I felt confident that this time I would receive some personalized attention. Perhaps even an interview with Commander Coakley.

As I approached the duty desk, I looked at the officer in charge and said, as matter-of-factly as I could, "I'm Lieutenant McCormick. I'm a survivor. . . ."

"Oh, a survivor, eh?" he said, handing me a "Survivor's Check-List," and saying, "next!"

That was the end of my "debriefing" about the saga of SS *William Gaston*.

After completing the usual "Officer Going On Leave Check-List," I was off to Fort Wayne by train again for a "survivor's leave" with my family and a few friends who were not in military service.

I found I was a kind of minor local celebrity, as the story of our encounter with a German U-boat in the South Atlantic had been carried by the press wire services at the time we landed in Miami and had appeared in Fort Wayne newspapers.

I was invited to describe my experiences at luncheon meetings of the local Kiwanis and Lions Clubs and at an assembly of employees of Indiana Service Corporation, the electrical and transit utility from which I was then on leave of absence. The president, who was a good friend and confidant of mine, gave me an honorarium which was roughly equivalent to a month's Navy pay.

At each such meeting I staged a little gag to lighten the story. I arranged with a friend of mine to sit in the back of the room carrying a pistol loaded with blank cartridges. At the most critical point of the story, on cue from me, he fired the gun to simulate the shock of the torpedoing.

During that visit there was no opportunity to go to Chicago to see my friend. She was on a late summer holiday at Sun Valley in Idaho. However, I did have a nice visit with her father, who was president and major shareholder of a large independent telephone company in Indiana. My older brother Cliff was one of his junior executives. I had had business dealings with her father before, starting in 1940. I began promising him that I would "drive carefully and not stay out too late with your daughter."

Chapter 15

1944 —
Aboard SS *Sandy Creek*

On 2 September 1944, following a 10-day leave in Fort Wayne, I reported in at the Armed Guard Center in Brooklyn, completed another "Officer Returning From Leave Check-List," and looked forward to a few nights back at the Henry Hudson Hotel in Manhattan, as it was the usual practice at the Center to place reporting personnel at the bottom of a roster to await assignment in sequence.

However, the Center apparently had a policy or practice of immediate duty for survivors in order to minimize the circulation of their stories. Accordingly, on the first morning, I was paged on the public address system and told to report to the Operations Office.

There the Officer on Duty said something like, "Lieutenant, in view of your recent experience, we have a good assignment for you. There's an ore carrier at a pier in Hoboken. She shuttles with bauxite cargoes between Venezuela and U.S. ports. You'll be back in the States every two weeks. Suppose you go over and take a look at the ship."

This in itself was a very unusual procedure.

I took subway and Hudson Tube trains to Hoboken, where I found the ship and went aboard. It was the dirtiest vessel I have ever seen before or since. It had been carrying bauxite for years, and the ore had left a permanent coating of brownish-yellow dust everywhere. The staterooms and mess halls were virtually unlivable.

I returned to Brooklyn, reported to the Operations Officer, and said something like, "Lieutenant, I've inspected the ore carrier, and it's filthy. If it's my *duty* to take that ship, I will naturally do so. But if you're trying to do me a favor, you're not."

He said, "Very well. Stand by outside while we look for another assignment."

In a little while I was paged again and told that I had been assigned to a new U.S. tanker, which had recently been launched by the Sun Shipbuilding & Drydock Co., at Chester, Pennsylvania.

The following morning I was assigned a crew of 26 men, including three Petty Officers (see crew list). We were photographed as a group, which was a new procedure, and were trucked to Penn Station, where we took a train to Chester and were provided Navy transportation to SS *Sandy Creek*, then undergoing final construction and outfitting at a pier in the Delaware River.

Sandy Creek, named after a minor battle of the Civil War, was one of the new T-2 class U.S. Merchant tankers. At 10,296 gross tons, it was nearly 50 percent larger than the Liberty ships. It had a large oil-burning turbine engine driving twin propellers on the stern, capable of speeds up to 16 to 18 knots and a cruising range of 12,600 nautical miles. The ship was owned by the War Shipping Administration and operated by Barber Asphalt Corporation of New York City.

The living quarters on *Sandy Creek* were larger and more comfortable than the Liberties. Officers and crews were lodged in a large midship house, while the galley and mess halls were located in the stern house. Unlike freighters, on which crews walked fore and aft on the main deck, T-2s were provided with steel open-grating catwalks connecting the midship house with the bow and stern.

At sea later, I was to learn that fully loaded tankers ride low in the water, and that, with heavy seas running, waves usually inundated the main deck, making the catwalk like a footbridge across a roaring river. On a dark stormy night, it was easy to forego a midnight snack in the mess hall aft rather than to make two unnerving crossings in the darkness on several hundred feet of spray-blown catwalk.

Sandy Creek's defensive armament was the same as on *William Gaston* — one 3.50-inch dual-purpose gun on the bow, one 5.38-inch dual-purpose gun on the stern, and eight 20-mm anti-aircraft guns.

The Master of *Sandy Creek* was Captain Randolph Karlsen, a mature Norwegian-American sailor who had gone to sea as a boy on a lobster boat off

---

Opposite: A September 1944 U.S. Navy photo at the Brooklyn Armed Guard Center of the author and 24 of the following 43 men who eventually served aboard the SS *Sandy Creek*: Gunnersmates Clyde F. Garrison, Joseph E. Pino, and Duane W. Hartman; Signalmen Clarence A. Wismeski, Raymond G. Christensen, Edward B. Westphal, Donald I. Miller, and Edward A. Kurlinkus; Seamen First Class Leo V. Barnes, Alfred J. Bohnsack, William R. Culp, Albert M. Dalton, Eugene A. Daniels, Herschel L. Day, Garland Dempsey, John T. Decker, Charles E. Dougherty, Robert E. Dunn, Edward C. Meadows, Edward Murray, Vernon Norris, Edward G. Orscheln, Harold D. Page, Soloman Pardue, Frank Parker, Zurga Franklin Dunno, Harvey Goodman, Raymond Kotecki, Herman H. Kraus, George Lazar, Roy T. Morris, Warren H. Myers, Elza C. Neece, Frank Alex Szoke, Robert M. Tipsword, Robert A. Tucker, Aloysius J. Kusinski, Louis Petrone, Ira E. Phinney, Minor E. Pierce, Wayne A. Rolen, Andy Kuchmaner, and Donald T. Miller. Unfortunately, after 47 years, the author is no longer able to associate names with faces.

The SS *Sandy Creek* was one of the new T-2 type of U.S. tankers, with a capacity of 6,000,000 gallons of petroleum products. (Photo, U.S. Navy, courtesy of National Archives)

Norway. The Chief Mate was Karl E. Tonnesen, also Norwegian-American. Almost in contrast, the Second Mate was a native New Yorker, John Hart, of Brooklyn, a graduate of Pratt Institute, who had suspended a promising career in commercial art to enroll in the King's Point Merchant Marine Academy. His keen intelligence and initiative enabled him to rise rapidly in the maritime service, and he later moved on to earn Chief Mate's and Master's licenses. Jack and I became very good friends and continued so until his death several years ago.

One of my most prized mementos of World War II is a large portrait which Jack painted of me, entitled "In An Atlantic Convoy, November 1944," while we both served aboard *Sandy Creek*.

On 28 September, following shakedown trials in Chesapeake Bay, *Sandy Creek* sailed independently for Aruba, Netherlands West Indies, to take on a cargo of aviation gasoline. Ironically, the same cargo was probably available from a Sunoco refinery at nearby Marcus Hook, Pennsylvania.

My Armed Guard log of that voyage contains the following entry, to which I have added locations parenthetically:

On 2 October, 0237 GMT (as we were approaching Mona Passage between the Dominican Republic and Puerto Rico), we received a distress message regarding a torpedoing at 23-17" N., 60-40" W. (northeast of San Juan), followed by a second message at 0305 GMT that the ship was being abandoned. Later same date, 0810 GMT, message received that another ship was being gunned off Atlantic City and later was reported beached there. In both instances, acknowledgements were heard from shore stations; hence, no further details are considered necessary in this report.

Sandy Creek arrived in the port of Aruba on 5 October to take on cargo. I have two specific recollections of our stay in Aruba — one pleasant and another not so pleasant. I have fond memories of the dinner I had one evening with Bernard P. Shearin, Jr., of Fort Wayne, son of a vice president of my prewar employer, Indiana Service Corporation, who was then employed by Standard Oil Company at its Aruba refinery. But my other memory of Aruba was the sickening sight of the blackened, abandoned hulls of several tankers which had been torpedoed and set afire earlier in the war and beached near the port.

After sailing from Aruba to New York, again independently, *Sandy Creek* joined a "fast" convoy to the United Kingdom — 26 ships, mostly troop carriers and tankers, and 10 escort vessels, speed 13 to 15 knots. It was immediately apparent that during the previous nine months, the U.S. and British Navies had made great progress in the organization and handling of

Atlantic convoys. In addition to greater speed and a higher ratio of escort vessels, the U.S. Navy was able to provide low-powered, short-wave portable Talk Between Ships (TBS) radios to all Merchant vessels. These made it possible to keep the entire convoy in constant communication. The Commodore could order and execute a change of course in a matter of seconds as compared with up to 30 minutes by the earlier blinker-light method. They also made it possible for Navy personnel on Merchant ships to "listen in" to messages between the Commodore and the escort vessels, like tuning in to a local police radio station in a high-crime area.

In addition to the convoy system, which was essentially defensive in purpose, the U.S. Navy also developed and deployed *offensive* anti-submarine forces. These were known as "killer groups" and consisted of one small aircraft carrier, a "baby flattop," usually a converted freighter, and a group of escort vessels. The planes from the carrier scouted for U-boats, while the escorts pursued and attacked them with depth charges. Thus, while the convoys were trying to avoid U-boats, the "killer groups" were seeking and destroying them. Eventually this combination began to gain the upper hand in the Battle of the Atlantic.

Besides walkie-talkie type radios, the newer U.S. Merchant ships were equipped with underwater high-frequency sound detectors mounted in the hull amidships on both port and starboard sides. These gave advance warning of approaching torpedoes as the sound of their propellers traveled faster underwater than the torpedoes themselves, which were rather slow as compared with artillery projectiles. The operation manual explained that if high-frequency sounds were picked up by either the port or starboard detectors, the ship should turn "hard over" to the opposite side, with a reasonable chance of evading the on-coming torpedo during its one- to two-minute run. Within a few months this "gimmick" probably saved *Sandy Creek*.

During the crossing, our escorts reported a number of U-boat contacts and dropped depth charges, especially in the Western Approaches to the United Kingdom. However, there were no apparent results, and the convoy arrived safely, *Sandy Creek* docking at Swansea, Wales, in the Bristol Channel, on 25 October. Several days were required to discharge our gasoline cargo, which enabled this wartime tourist from Indiana to spend a day in Cardiff, the capital of Wales.

* * *

On 29 October, *Sandy Creek* joined another west-bound convoy consisting of 23 vessels and 6 escorts. As usual, the Merchant vessels were not assigned a port of destination until 24 to 48 hours before arrival, when orders of the War Shipping Administration were signaled to each Merchant Master by the

By late 1944, Allied North Atlantic convoy operations had become very sophisticated. All of the Merchant ships had been equipped with walkie-talkie type radios, and U.S. Navy blimps had been added to escort forces to act as lookouts for U-boats. (Photos, U.S. Navy, courtesy of National Archives)

Convoy Commodore.

Selfishly, I always wanted to return to New York, and my ships always did, although many others were routed to Boston, Philadelphia, Baltimore, and other East Coast ports.

Upon arrival at various piers in the port of New York, and after setting Navy crew watch schedules in charge of the Senior Petty Officer Gunner's Mate, I would put on my dress blue uniform and go ashore for both business and pleasure. This included a visit to the Armed Guard Center to turn in my voyage report and draw pay, then a trip to a Chinese laundry, and then to the Henry Hudson Hotel, where I usually checked in when my ship was in port.

* * *

During the period 15 November through 12 December, *Sandy Creek* completed another round-trip voyage, in convoys, between New York and Liverpool, England, returning to New York. On this trip there were several developments worthy of mention. For the first time we carried deck cargo in addition to aviation gasoline — 10 or 12 P-47 U.S. Thunderbolt fighter-bombers to be delivered to England. Also, U-boat activity in the Western Approaches on 23, 24, and 25 November was much greater than on the previous trip, and as we tied up in the Mersey River between Liverpool and Birkenhead, an escorting British Corvette sailed up the river with flags flying, a broom mounted on the stack, and its bow staved in, indicating the ramming and sinking of a U-boat the previous night. In spite of these developments, this wartime tourist from Indiana was able to spend several days in Edinburgh, Scotland, one of the most charming and best-preserved historical cities in the world. It was an unforgettable experience to walk up the Royal Mile from Mary Queen of Scots' Holyrood Palace, past the Norman Chapel of Saint Margaret, St. Giles' Cathedral, and the old Whitehorse Tavern — all monuments of the sixteenth and seventeenth centuries — to ancient Edinburgh Castle on Castle rock overlooking the city.

In contrast to Brazil, where it had been necessary to obtain police permits to travel between Santos and San Paulo, in Great Britain, which was far more vulnerable to enemy spies and saboteurs, it was possible for anyone to purchase railway tickets to go anywhere, with no questions asked. I considered this a unique affirmation of democracy and personal freedom, even under wartime conditions.

* * *

After one trip in the fall of 1944, I met Captain Karlsen at the Port Director's Office in the Whitehall Building in Lower Manhattan, where convoy conferences were always held. We were told the *Sandy Creek* was to join another "UK Fast" convoy, scheduled to depart at mid-morning the following day. Meanwhile, the ship had been loaded with aviation gasoline and aircraft deck cargo and was then riding at anchor near the Statue of Liberty.

I decided to remain ashore for another night at the Henry Hudson. Early the next morning I took the subway to Bowling Green to catch a water taxi out to the ship from the dock near the Staten Island Ferry terminal.

After we were underway we saw that another convoy was then arriving, with ships passing in single file to the port side of our convoy. Suddenly, the air was filled with flames and smoke as an empty inbound tanker scraped against a fully loaded tanker at anchor, rupturing the latter's tanks and setting off an enormous fire. The flaming fuel spread across the harbor and badly damaged other vessels. SS *Seven Pines*, a sister ship of ours and operated by the same line, was virtually destroyed. *Sandy Creek* was undamaged and sailed more or less on time with the rest of the convoy.

Later I wondered, and still wonder, how and even *if* the New York media covered that story. At the time the press was operating under a code which discouraged publication of any news which would "give aid and comfort to the enemy." Yet, the towering smoke was viewed by thousands of witnesses on shore and no doubt relayed by word of mouth to the entire city. How *did* the press handle the story? I still don't know.

While in New York on another visit I made a date to take the train down to Washington, D.C., to visit WAVE Lieutenant Marjorie Lytle, USNR, who had been a friend of mine at Great Lakes but had been transferred to the Navy Department in Washington.

After I arrived at her apartment, Marge told me she planned to prepare a home-cooked meal and asked me to go to a nearby grocery store and pick up a pound of butter, which I did.

After dinner I caught an evening train back to New York. Some days later when *Sandy Creek* was at sea again, I discovered that I still had Marge's U.S. food ration book in an inside pocket of my dress-blue uniform. I wonder why I never heard from her again.

During my next layover in New York I received a dinner invitation from Mr. and Mrs. Phil Porterfield, old friends from Fort Wayne who were then living in nearby Larchmont, New York. Having previously learned something about wartime shortages on the "home front," I persuaded the steward on *Sandy Creek* to give me several pounds of butter from the ship's stores. I took those with me as hostess gifts and found that at that time butter was more appreciated than flowers.

* * *

On returning from one voyage I received a letter from my brother Cliff suggesting that, since I was back at sea and presumably had free time, I should consider writing a book about my experience on *William Gaston*. Fat chance! With that memory still fresh in my mind, and then riding a gasoline tanker, I was too uptight to even *read* a book! I did think of a title, however — *Two Years Behind the Mast* — but I didn't get around to writing it until 40 years later.

On 14 December *Sandy Creek* again sailed from New York, this time independently, bound to Gibraltar for orders. I recall well that we were in Gibraltar on Christmas day, 25 December 1944. While in that port I was able to cross the border to La Linea, Spain, thus ticking off another country on my grand tour, much in the same way a bird watcher checks off a new species on his lifetime bird list. I also visited the British Navy Operations Office, where I inquired whether there was anything interesting to see on Gibraltar. The officer in charge assured me, "There's *nothing* to see in this God-forsaken place."

Walking back to the ship I passed what appeared to be a tiny park. Upon investigation, I found an old plaque identifying the place as Trafalgar Cemetery — the final resting place of British sailors who died with Lord Nelson in the Battle of Trafalgar, off the Spanish coast, on 21 October 1805. I felt it was *well* worth seeing.

On 26 December *Sandy Creek* departed Gibraltar, again independently, passing through the Straits bound to Augusta, Sicily, for orders, then in convoy to Taranto, Italy, to discharge our aviation gasoline cargo destined for the U.S. Army Air Forces base at Bari, Italy.

Taranto is located under the heel of the Italian "boot" and had a reputation for being very volatile politically. While there, I had an experience which still fills me with mixed emotions. It was New Year's Eve, and after *Sandy Creek* had tied up at a pier, I joined several of the Merchant officers for celebration drinks at a waterfront bar. We all drank too much, and I more than I could handle. After midnight we started to walk back to the ship. But I became tired and sleepy, and when I could walk no farther, I sat down on a sidewalk bench and fell asleep.

The next thing I knew, I awakened with a start in a strange environment. I was in the interior of a large cavernous building, lying on a cot, with a coarse blanket over me, fully dressed except for my shoes and hat, which I found on the floor nearby. I sat up, arose, and walked to the faint night light of a nearby opened, glassless window. Peering out and down I found that I was on the fourth or fifth floor of what appeared to be an abandoned waterfront warehouse. I had no idea how I had gotten there.

Returning to the cot, I sat down and, through the fog of my hangover, tried to evaluate my situation. I had to conclude that I must be in the hands of a friend or friends. How else could I explain the cot and the blanket? I had no idea of the time of night, and because I was ill and tired, I tried to get a little

Allied ships in the harbor at Gibraltar, as viewed from the Rock, with the end of the only runway at the right. (Photo, courtesy of Imperial War Museum, London)

more fitful sleep while I awaited morning.

Just before daybreak, I roused myself again, put on my shoes and hat, and decided to face whatever lie ahead on New Year's Day, 1 January 1945.

In the early morning light I groped my way to the other end of the building, where I found an old concrete-and-steel spiral staircase leading down to the first floor. There I came face to face with an elderly Italian man, who was the caretaker and who apparently had found and befriended me the night before. It was an almost classical confrontation. He could speak no English and I could speak no Italian. We nodded at each other in a kind of mute understanding. I reached into my pocket to offer money, but he would not accept it. Finally, we shook hands and I walked out.

For more than 40 years since I have assumed that, although Italy and America had lately been enemies, the old man probably had Italian relatives in the United States and considered Americans as friends. Had he had other motives, this Hoosier tourist might well have been found floating in the Gulf of Taranto.

On 2 January 1945, *Sandy Creek* sailed from Taranto, independently to Gibraltar, and then convoyed, one ship and one escort, to 10° West longitude, and then independently to New York.

During the long voyage home, I had much opportunity to contemplate that 1944 had been a very eventful year for me — two trips to Italy, two trips to the United Kingdom, a long voyage to South America with stopovers in Brazil, Argentina, and other countries, not to mention a torpedoing and several other adventures. I wondered what 1945 would bring.

Sandy Creek arrived in the Port of New York on 16 January, and although the Armed Guard was eligible for leave, we decided to stay aboard for another voyage. Regrettably, my friend Second Mate Jack Hart took leave, and I was not to see him again until several years after the war.

Chapter 16

1945 —
Aboard SS *Sandy Creek*

By the beginning of 1945, the Allies were well on their way toward winning World War II against the Axis powers. In Europe, they had already secured the surrender of Italy in September 1943, had occupied both Northern and Southern France in 1944, and by January 1945 were poised for the final thrust into Germany, with the Russians attacking on the Eastern Front. In the Pacific, U.S. Forces had already recaptured major positions taken by the Japanese in 1942, and were then "island hopping" toward the Philippines and the mainland of Japan.

Against that background, frequent fast convoys of troopships, tankers, and freighters were operating continuously between the U.S. and the United Kingdom and Mediterranean. Between 5 February and 5 March, *Sandy Creek* completed another round-trip voyage, in convoys, between New York and Liverpool, again carrying aviation gasoline and a deck cargo of P-47 Thunderbolt fighter-bombers. U-boat activity in the North Atlantic appeared to have lessened somewhat.

My most agreeable recollection of that voyage was the fact that it afforded me a long-awaited opportunity to spend several days in London. I saw all of the tourist sights — Westminster Abbey, Buckingham Palace, the Tower of London, St. Paul's Cathedral, Covent Garden Opera, which had been badly bombed, and *even* Madame Tussaud's Wax Museum.

Although the worst of German air raids on London had ended several years earlier, thousands and thousands of Londoners were sleeping on makeshift bedding in the underground subway stations — which, incidentally, are much deeper than in New York and other U.S. cities. The crowds consisted primarily of women, children, and the elderly, as most men were in the military or in war-related industries. It was a kind of historic preview of modern homelessness in major U.S. metropolises.

* * *

Back in New York in early March, the Armed Guard crew on *Sandy Creek* had an opportunity to make what turned out to be a rather fateful decision. Actually, it was a decision I had to make, but I asked the Petty Officers to give me a consensus from the crew. At that time, we had been aboard *Sandy Creek* for over six months and were entitled to apply for leave and go home. On the other hand, the weather was cold and wet, we were scheduled to make another round trip to England, and we all felt that a leave in April's spring weather would be more agreeable. Therefore, I told the Armed Guard Center in Brooklyn that our crew would stay aboard *Sandy Creek* for another voyage.

It was always a pleasure to return to New York, pick up mail from home, and spend an evening or two with other Armed Guard officers at the Henry Hudson Hotel. One night I picked up a few New York newspapers and a copy of *Life* magazine to take back to the ship. That particular issue carried a photo feature about the young American social set enjoying the ski resorts of Colorado. It included a very good picture of my Fort Wayne-Chicago girlfriend.

Sandy Creek was scheduled to take on both aviation gasoline and a deck cargo of P-47s at separate piers on the New Jersey side of the Hudson River. During the period 7-8 March the New York harbor became fogbound. We were unable to move the ship and got behind in our loading operations for a convoy scheduled to sail on 9 March. As a result, we missed the departure of the convoy and became a minor problem for Naval authorities.

On the morning of 10 March, Captain Karlsen and I were called to the office of the Port Director in lower Manhattan and asked to stand by while a decision was being made regarding the ship's orders. We sat on a bench in an anteroom and listened to a series of discussions and telephone calls regarding the Navy's plans for *Sandy Creek*.

As we could overhear, there were a number of possible options. We could sail as soon as possible and try to overtake the convoy. We could be ordered independently to England or the Mediterranean, but that apparently was deemed too risky. We could be held over for the next fast convoy to England in about a week, but that appeared to be wasteful, or we could be routed independently through the Panama Canal to the Pacific theater, but the P-47s already on board were really needed for ground troop support in Europe, not the Pacific.

I'll never forget overhearing the final telephone conversation, apparently with Washington, which revealed the decision regarding our dilemma. An officer on the phone said, "Okay, now let's review that. *Sandy Creek* will sail independently to Casablanca to unload the planes, sail independently through the Med and Suez to India to discharge cargo, then stand by for orders. Roger."

Thus, by a quirk of fate, instead of waiting 30 days for leave, it was destined to be nearly a year before we returned to the States!

At that time, *Sandy Creek* was riding at anchor in the Hudson River off the 79th Street Boat Basin, with new orders to sail at 10 p.m., on 10 March. That, at least, was convenient for me, as it gave me an opportunity for another farewell party with the constantly changing Navy "gang" at the Henry Hudson on West 58th Street. I left the hotel about 9 p.m. and took a taxicab to 79th Street and a water taxi out to the ship, where I received a report that all Navy personnel were on board.

As *Sandy Creek* sailed down the Hudson toward Ambrose Light en route to Africa and India, I stood on the port wing of the bridge, watching the dimmed-out skyline of Manhattan disappearing behind us and wondering how long it would be before we saw New York again.

At about midnight, still awake in my cabin, I heard a kind of muffled explosion in the engine room below. I ran up to the wheel house on the bridge, where the Captain had already joined the Mate on Watch. The Captain was speaking by voice tube to the Chief Engineer who had gone to the engine room. The Chief reported that the ship had blown a steam valve and that the crew could fix it, but the engine would have to be shut down, possibly for several hours.

At that time, *Sandy Creek* was about 50 miles east of Ambrose Light, at about the 100-fathom curve (600 feet of ocean), a favorite waiting place for U-boats. The minutes dragged on like hours as we paced the wheel house and wings of the bridge in silence. Periodically, hammering in the engine room would set up a vibration in the hull and cause the sonic torpedo detectors to screech loudly. Finally, this became unbearable, and the Captain turned off the system, as it was useless unless the ship was underway.

From time to time, I would walk over to the "radio shack" on the boat deck and join the Operator in listening to radio signals. We heard the regular military broadcasts on a short-wave marine band, and long-wave AM programs featuring late-night dance music from Manhattan hotel ballrooms. New York seemed so close and yet so faraway.

Finally, sometime around 2 a.m., the Chief Engineer reported that the repairs had been completed and that the engine could be restarted. Within a few minutes, mercifully, the ship was underway again, to the great relief of all on board. In fact, although we were heading out into the Atlantic independently, there was considerable exhilaration just to be moving again. I literally fell into my bunk after a nearly 20-hour day.

Early in the morning of 20 March, *Sandy Creek* was approaching the port of

Casablanca, French Morocco. As usual, I was in the wheel house, with binoculars, trying to pick up the first sight of land. The Chief Mate was on watch. Suddenly, the torpedo detector on the port side started shrieking a high-frequency sound. The Chief immediately shouted to the helmsman, "Hard right!"

As the shriek continued to grow in volume, the ship began to make a long, slow turn to starboard. Almost in terror, we waited in silence. After 60 to 90 nerve-shattering seconds, the sound suddenly ceased momentarily, then resumed again on the starboard side, finally diminishing into silence. Without doubt, *Sandy Creek* had been fired at with a torpedo, which missed us by either crossing our turning bow or running too deep in the water and passing under our keel. Later, ashore in Casablanca, the Captain of another U.S. tanker, approaching the harbor, told us his ship had picked up the same sounds.

Casablanca, with its ancient Moorish architecture, was the most exotic place I had ever seen up to that time. The city had taken on a romantic image for most Americans — the place where Allied Forces landed in November 1942 in their first amphibious assault in the Afro-European theater; the site where President Roosevelt, Prime Minister Churchill, and French Generals DeGaulle and Giraud had conferred in January 1943; and the setting for the classic U.S. motion picture, *Casablanca*, starring Humphrey Bogart and Ingrid Bergman.

While sightseeing in Casablanca, I had perhaps the most embarrassing experience of my wartime travels. While strolling through the old Medinah, I attracted a gang of teen-age Arab street urchins. Using a kind of pidgin English, the leader indicated that he wanted to buy my wristwatch. I had no interest in selling it, but out of curiosity I asked his offer. He said something like, "hunna doll," and revealed some folded U.S. currency in his palm. Meanwhile, the gang continued to dart around me and indicated they were concerned about the gendarmes. Finally, feeling I could easily replace the watch, I removed it from my wrist and exchanged it for the currency, after which the gang ran down the street. Only then did I discover that I had fallen for what I learned later was one of the oldest tricks in that part of the world. I had a $10 bill folded in such a way that it appeared to be $100! Both irate and amused, I recognized that I had sold for $10 a watch that had cost me about $10 in a post exchange. I was really out nothing — except some of my self-respect!

After the P-47s had been unloaded in Casablanca, *Sandy Creek* sailed northward, then through the Straits of Gibraltar, and through the Mediterranean to the Suez Canal. At Port Said, Captain Karlsen and I were able to go ashore to clear the ship's passage through the canal and to have lunch at an old Egyptian hotel overlooking the Mediterranean and a statue of Ferdinand de Lesseps, the French builder of the canal, looking out to sea.

Our first-time passage of the canal was a tourist's delight. Unlike the

Pannama Canal, which utilizes a series of locks to lift and lower ships across that isthmus, the Suez is almost a "natural" sea-level canal, which cuts through a hundred miles of rolling desert to connect the Mediterranean to the Red Sea and Indian Ocean.

Sandy Creek also put into the port of Suez at the southern terminus of the canal. I don't remember why, unless it was to complete paperwork for our transit. At that time the canal was operated by a private corporation, the Suez Canal Company, and ships' operators were responsible for paying tolls. Captain Karlsen and I went ashore, and I was able to add Suez to my growing list of exotic ports of call.

* * *

After passage through the canal, the Bitter Lakes, and the Red Sea, *Sandy Creek* sailed eastward across the Indian Ocean to Colombo, Ceylon, for orders, then to Madras on the east coast of India, where we discharged part of the cargo, and finally on to Calcutta on the Hooghly River, to discharge the balance. It was then mid-April 1945.

These large Indian cities were, to me, even more exotic than Casablanca, Port Said, and Suez, and the architecture was even more oriental. However, there was an important and welcome difference. Because India had so long been colonized by the British, English was the language of diplomacy and commerce, and *The Times* of India, in English, was the Eastern equivalent of *The Times* of London. It was possible to move about anywhere, because there were no language barriers.

My principal recollections of India were, on the one hand, the extreme poverty and hunger of most of the people, and, on the other, the abundance of livestock, particularly Brahman cattle, sacred to the Hindus, wandering through the streets, stopping the traffic, and grazing on the vegetation in the public parks. It was all incomprehensible to a Western mind.

* * *

Several of my experiences in India were right out of an old travelogue movie. One day in Madras I joined others in watching a street show staged by an old Hindu entertainer who carried two baskets, one containing a cobra and the other a mongoose, which are ancient enemies in that part of the world. When a sufficient crowd had gathered, he emptied both baskets on the sidewalk and allowed the cobra and mongoose to confront each other in an eerie sparring match. Although such meetings often end fatally for one of the adversaries, usually the cobra, the showman was able to "stop the fight" at a critical juncture in order that his performers could meet again another time.

Before moving on, the Hindu solicited and received coins from the small crowd.

While on a walking tour of Madras I came upon a huge Hindu temple covered with tiers of sculpted statues and other ornamentation. A Hindu boy at the entrance, anticipating a tip of a few annas, escorted me through the ornate structure and led me to a stone figure which he identified as "Mahatma," sensing correctly that Gandhi was the only Hindu with whom an American serviceman would be familiar. Some days later, while in Calcutta, I had a very different experience under similar circumstances. I ventured into a beautiful Moslem mosque, not knowing that nonbelievers in Allah were forbidden to do so. I failed to remove my shoes, which was considered a desecration, and was unceremoniously ushered out by several angry Moslem men in turbans whose message was clear even though their words were not.

While at the Harbormaster's Office in Calcutta, I became acquainted with a young British Naval officer, who invited me to join him for a drink at the English cricket club located at the edge of town. We made the trip in individual rickshaws pulled by barefooted Hindu men. The facility looked like an American country club but with polo and cricket fields. Well-dressed women and men, in uniform and mufti, both sat at outdoor tables drinking tea or whiskey, in marked contrast to the general poverty of Calcutta.

While in India, I purchased at street bazaars a few small hand-carved ivory and ebony elephants and Hindu gods, which I still have.

After discharging the last of our cargo in Calcutta, there was then a question as to our future orders. To those of us on *Sandy Creek*, the most logical course would have been to sail to the Persian Gulf, pick up new cargo, and deliver it to Europe or even America. In our speculations, we were half right. We were ordered to the Persian Gulf to pick up cargo, but, through some Allied agreement, we were "loaned" to the British Navy for the purpose of delivering petroleum products to bases in Egypt, Aden, Ceylon, and the principal cities of Australia.

Beginning in April and continuing until December 1945, *Sandy Creek*, and everyone aboard, was on a kind of Indian Ocean treadmill. We made seven trips into the Persian Gulf to pick up cargoes at Abadan, Iran, and Bahrein Island off Saudi Arabia, for delivery to Suez, Egypt; Aden, Yemen; Trincomalee, Ceylon; and Melbourne, Sydney, Brisbane, Townsville, and Darwin, Australia. On one trip, we actually circumnavigated Australia, counterclockwise.

During the long, seemingly endless sea passages between the Persian Gulf and Australian cities, daylight hours became monotonous, and some recreation was essential. Aboard *Sandy Creek* there were only five bridge players among the officers — two Mates, two Engineers, and myself. However, because the day was divided into six four-hour watch periods, and off-watch time was usually reserved for sleeping, it was not always easy to find a "fourth for bridge." When possible, we usually began during the 12 to 4 p.m. watch and concluded it between 4 o'clock and the evening meal. Two or three players would have changed during the game, and reconciling bets was impossible.

On any ship at sea, days of the week gradually lose their meaning. On *Sandy Creek*, throughout 1945, even weeks or months became lost in a never-ending cycle of days and nights, nearly all of them at sea because of the fast turn-around of tankers.

Although I have ship's logs and voyage reports of that period, I can no longer think of events in any kind of chronological order. Instead, I will simply record some of the principal experiences and observations which remain with me to this day.

First of all, the Persian Gulf, aside from its wealth in underground oil, was then literally the armpit of the whole world. The temperature in summer in Abadan was unbelievable — 130° to 140° Fahrenheit at noon at the U.S. Army Air Forces base. Poverty in the town was beyond description, dramatized by a small stream in which the townspeople — men, women, and children — bathed, washed clothes and dishes, and urinated and defecated, forming a continuous lineup along the banks.

After two or three visits, most crewmen of *Sandy Creek*, normally eager for shore leave, wouldn't even go ashore in the Persian Gulf despite their long days at sea. That was the only area of the World I visited where I never had anything to eat or drink while ashore. Nevertheless, the bazaar in Abadan offered wares which were both exotic and primitive, such as crude piles of untreated Persian Lamb skins.

One day in Abadan I stopped to watch an Iranian potter as he shaped a large and lovely water jar on his potter's wheel. When he was finished, I tried to indicate that I would like to buy it, offering U.S. currency from my pocket. Standing up, he indicated that he had no interest in my money but would like to have my shirt, whereupon I removed it and gave it to him. I carried the pottery back to the ship in khaki trousers and underwear top — hardly the "uniform of the day!"

On one trip to the Persian Gulf, I was able to hitchhike a ride in an Army Jeep from Abadan to Basra, Iraq, across the Shatt-al-Arab River, passing through date palm and olive tree groves to a city which resembled, to me, an old woodcut out of an early edition of the Bible.

* * *

If possible, Bahrein Island was even more primitive than Abadan and Basra. There were no docking facilities whatever, and it was necessary for tankers to anchor offshore and take on cargo through pipelines extending out from the land on floating pontoons. I was able to get a ride to shore in an oil company launch and visit the small town which had sprung up around the oil terminal. I discovered there a rather amusing phenomenon. In all the seaports from North Africa to India, natives around the docks were trying to obtain wristwatches or bed linens from sailors through purchase or barter. On Bahrein Island, due to the vagaries of the wartime trade, there apparently was a surplus of wristwatches, and natives in loincloths and bare feet were trying to sell or exchange them for bedsheets!

While in the Middle East we witnessed another rather strange but fairly frequent practice. Although shops in the bazaars were open for business throughout the day, trade would cease completely five times daily while proprietors and clerks knelt on prayer rugs and bowed toward Mecca.

* * *

On 7 May 1945 — V-E Day in Europe — *Sandy Creek* happened to be in Aden, along with a number of British ships. When the surrender of Germany was announced on radio by the BBC, the British seamen literally went wild. As part of their celebration, they used their ship's guns like fireworks. After nearly six years of war and the near destruction of England, they had a lot to celebrate.

But for *Sandy Creek* it was still business as usual. On the next trip to Australia, we had an experience worth mentioning. During a storm in the Indian Ocean, one of the Navy crewmen, Signalman Edward B. Westphal, USNR, was thrown against a stanchion and broke his collarbone. I learned then and have never forgotten that it is called the clavicle. We had no doctor on board and were then nearly three weeks out of Melbourne. The boy was in considerable pain and faced a prospect of improper knitting and possible rebreaking and resetting of the bone.

Under our orders, *Sandy Creek* was instructed to break radio silence only once every three days to give our position and a brief weather report. I persuaded the Captain that on our next radio transmission we should add a brief report that we had an injured sailor on board. He was reluctant, but finally agreed to let me add the message.

Later that night we received a special radio signal to *Sandy Creek*, ordering us to proceed to a location approximately on the equator at about 75° East longitude. The Captain was annoyed and skeptical because his navigation charts showed nothing at that position, and he was concerned about being late in arriving in Melbourne.

Early the following morning, as we approached the location, I was in the wheel house with the Captain and Chief Mate, all scanning the eastern horizon with binoculars, looking for a sight of land or possibly a rendevousing British

Naval vessel. In a little while a fringe of palm trees loomed in the distance at a point where there was no land or island shown on the navigation chart. As we approached closer, a blinker light began to signal us from the shore. Ironically, Signalman Westphal was the only man on board who could read Morse code by blinker, and he had to be assisted up to the bridge to receive the message.

Sandy Creek was instructed to reduce speed and to approach on a very specific northeasterly course. As we neared, we could see a large and lovely atoll. We sailed through a channel in the horseshoe-shaped chain and dropped anchor in a spacious natural harbor. We soon learned that the place was called Adu Atoll, which had been discovered many years before, but the British had not shown it on their navigation charts because it was conceived as an ideal secret anchorage for the British Far Eastern Fleet.

Although the Atoll was one of the most primitive places imaginable (one of the islands was a leper colony), it also had some very sophisticated wartime facilities and personnel — a small medical clinic with an electric generator and a modern weather station, manned by several British doctors and meteorologists. They were actually able to X-ray and reset Westphal's clavicle. And, by contrast, they prepared tea with water heated over a fire of palm logs. Unbelievable!

But there were also contrasts to all of this. On one trip, while awaiting clearance to the docks at Abadan, Captain Karlsen and I were again invited to have tea — this time by the British Harbormaster, whose base was the royal yacht of the King of Iraq, which had been loaned or commandeered for the duration of the war. We were picked up by the King's launch and taken aboard the yacht, which was the most luxurious vessel I had ever seen before or since — gleaming white hull and bulkheads, mahogany rails, hardwood decks, and polished brass on the outside; and oriental carpets, crystal chandeliers, oil paintings, and even wood or coal-burning fireplaces in the inner quarters. Fortunately, the British "tea" turned out to be Australian brandy, which was much appreciated in those days in that part of the world.

We were told that the yacht at one time had been owned by William Wrigley, the American industrialist. However, my research in recent years has revealed that information to have been inaccurate. According to the Scottish Record Office in Edinburgh, the vessel had been built in 1923 in Clydebank for British Lord Tredegar, Duke of Sutherland, and was named "Sans Peur." In the 1930s it was sold to the King of Iraq and was renamed "Faisal I."

Weather conditions in the Gulf were really weird. When we did a little personal laundry it was our practice to hang it over a rail to dry in the sun. If the wind was blowing off the desert, the clothes would be dry in a few minutes. However, if the wind changed and blew off the Gulf, the clothes would be damp again just as quickly.

On the long, tedious trips to and from Australia, we had little to break the monotony except our observations of the natural world around us. I was fascinated to watch porpoises alternately breaking water and diving along our bow, like untrained dogs chasing automobile wheels on land. And, as the old song says, "On the Road to Mandalay . . . the flying fishes play." They really do, like amphibious birds rising periodically from the sea and flying above the waves for 20 to 30 feet or more, with wings flapping in the spray. And then, at night, there were the stars and constellations. On our long shuttles north and south, we saw the Big Dipper and the Southern Cross in alternate months. In mid-July, while *Sandy Creek* was sailing along Australia's southern coast, snow fell and accumulated on the main deck.

On the long southbound trips, often in bad weather, with the tanker loaded to her gunwales and riding low in the water, it was easy for me to forego the late-night snacks in the mess hall and thus eliminate the wind-swept, nerve-wracking trips to the stern house in darkness over the "Bridge of Sighs" catwalk with seas roaring across the main deck a few feet below.

On one trip the ship's refrigeration system broke down. After several days, the Captain ordered all meat thrown over the side, and for a week or ten days we had to subsist on canned goods and bread.

In Australian cities *Sandy Creek* could take on new stores of fresh meats, vegetables, and fruits. In the Asian ports such commodities were virtually nonexistent for Western tastes.

The only pleasures of this whole period were our periodic calls at the major seaports of Australia. As is well known, Sydney has one of the most beautiful harbors in the world. I was especially impressed with the city's relaxed lifestyle, in particular, people commuting back and forth to work by ferryboat from suburban towns located along the perimeter of the large harbor. I also visited Taronga Park on an island in the harbor, which had a beautiful zoo housing kangaroos, koala bears, and other Australian wildlife.

Melbourne was also a delight, especially on one trip which coincided with the running of the Melbourne Cup Race. Although, as a U.S. Midwesterner, I always assumed that the Kentucky Derby was the greatest horse race in the world, I was enormously impressed when I attended the 1945 Melbourne Cup at Flemington Race Course. Although the horses ran clockwise, which seemed odd, there was no point in being underimpressed by the 100,000-plus attendance or by the symphonic band, which played classical music in the infield between races.

During this period I became involved in what would now be recognized as a "Catch-22" situation. One day in Melbourne, we received mail from the States, which included new orders for me to "detach yourself from your present duty and proceed to Philadelphia, Pa., for assignment to the Office of Naval Officer Procurement." The next paragraph was the catch: "These orders are subject to the condition that a qualified replacement is available for your present assignment." Find a replacement in the Persian Gulf or Australia? I hadn't even *seen* another U.S. Naval officer for over six months!

During this latter period, *Sandy Creek* delivered another cargo to Aden, a place which never ceased to amaze me. The townspeople were dumping their garbage into the harbor, which attracted schools of sharks, giant stingrays, water snakes, and other scavengers of the sea, churning the water around the ship. Outside of town a native company was "harvesting" salt by using windmills to pump seawater into vast sand flats for evaporation by the broiling sun.

One day, while walking through town with an officer from the ship and engaged in an animated conversation, I suddenly became aware that we were standing still, and almost unconsciously I wondered why. I looked up and saw that all traffic was being halted by a long camel train passing through town. I said to my friend, "My God, we've got to get out of this part of the world. I don't even notice camel trains anymore!"

On 2 September 1945, when Japanese senior officers surrendered to General MacArthur on the USS *Missouri* in Tokyo Bay, the *Sandy Creek* was at sea in the Indian Ocean, traveling between Melbourne and Abadan. It was, of course, very thrilling news, although it didn't seem to affect us very much. We were still on a routine haul, carrying oil to Australia. That was to continue for three more months.

On one occasion, while *Sandy Creek* was again loading cargo in Abadan, the British Harbormaster told us that the Moslem world was then observing the Fast of Ramadan, which commemorates the first revelations of Allah to Muhammad in the seventh century. He told us that Moslems are forbidden to eat, drink, smoke, or enjoy any other worldly pleasures between sunrise and sunset during that season, that they become very hostile to nonbelievers in Islam, and that we should be very circumspect toward them while we were ashore. Fortunately, there were no unpleasant instances, perhaps because we had few social contacts with the local residents. However, as we have learned in recent years, Iran can be a very unfriendly place for Westerners.

While ashore one day, I happened to see two tattered newspapers rolled up and left on a public bench near the loading dock. One was *The Times of India*, published in Calcutta; the other was *Our Sunday Visitor*, a weekly paper of the Catholic Diocese of Fort Wayne, published in Huntington, Indiana!

On the same visit to Abadan, I had one of my most poignant experiences of the entire war. After nearly two years at sea, I received a "Dear Cap" (family nickname) letter from my hometown girlfriend in Chicago, whom I still hoped to marry after the war. She told me that her widowed father was announcing her engagement and approaching marriage to another USNR officer. In spite of my disappointment and pain, I felt there was a certain ironic humor in the letter, which seemed to make the plan sound like it was her father's idea —

which was not the case, of course.

Because of delays in wartime mail deliveries, I knew that any response I might make would not reach her until after the wedding, which seemed awkward. I chose to write a letter to her father, asking him in my best stiff-upper-lip style to give his daughter my very best wishes.

Although I was to see her father a few times after the war, he did not write me a letter until ten years later. In 1955, my postwar business career had made modest progress, and my picture appeared in *The New York Times*. He wrote me a fatherly-like letter of congratulations, which I appreciated and still have in my files. Incidentally, as a kind of "it's a small world" aside, at that time my prewar rival in romance, Ken Ryan, was a co-worker and good friend of mine at General Electric Company in Electronics Park, Syracuse, N.Y.

In late September 1945, when we were again under way on another trip to Australia, I went to the stern of *Sandy Creek* and dropped her picture from *Life* into the ship's wake in the Indian Ocean.

* * *

At this interval it may be appropriate to mention that because tankers can load or discharge cargo in a matter of hours instead of the days required by freighters, the crew of *Sandy Creek* had relatively short shore leaves and virtually no social life in the ports we visited.

In Australia there was a whole generation of young women whose male friends were away serving with ANZAC Forces in the Mediterranean theater. At the same time, thousands of American servicemen visited Australia briefly enroute to the island-hopping operations in the Western Pacific.

In Brisbane, in the same hotel where General McArthur had once had his headquarters, I had a mutually meaningless one-night stand with one of the local "drugstore cowgirls." But, in Melbourne, which we visited several times, I enjoyed a friendly, platonic relationship with a young woman who had married an American GI early in the war, but hadn't heard from him since his outfit had sailed for Guadalcanal in November 1942. In the human casualties of war, there are no statistics on broken hearts.

* * *

Sometime during October, as I recall, the U.S. Navy Department issued an order to all Armed Guard Commanders on Merchant ships still at sea to throw all ammunition overboard in at least 100 fathoms of water. At the time, that seemed rather ironic, as we previously had been warned not to expend too much ammunition in target practice. However, it no doubt was necessary as the considerable quantity of projectiles on Merchant ships would have posed a major handling and storage problem back in the States. Accordingly, we dumped *Sandy Creek's* ammunition in the middle of the Indian Ocean.

On 6 November, while again in Melbourne, I was able to detach eight members of the Armed Guard crew who were then qualified for honorable discharge from the Navy. They were turned over to U.S. Navy authorities in Australia for transportation to the United States. On 7 November *Sandy Creek* sailed north again for its seventh voyage to the Persian Gulf.

Finally, on 11 December 1945, I and 13 members of the Navy Gun Crew were detached from *Sandy Creek* at Port Said, Egypt, and assigned passage on the American troopship USS *General W.F. Hase* for transportation to the United States through the Mediterranean and across the Atlantic. The balance of the Navy crew, in the charge of Gunnersmate Joseph E. Pino, USNR, of Providence, Rhode Island, remained aboard the ship, eventually returning to the States from Australia via the Panama Canal, arriving in Norfolk, Virginia, in March 1946.

Our transfer in the Suez Canal from *Sandy Creek* to *General Hase* was both embarrassing and amusing for me. Our Navy gunners were able to walk up the gangplank carrying all their worldly goods in their seabags. However, I explained to the troopship's Officer of the Watch that I had to transfer several large cartons (ammunition boxes as big as appliance crates) from one ship to the other. As a result, he had to call for steam on deck and use the cargo booms to effect the transfer as hundreds of U.S. troops watched from the ship's rails.

The Army officer had the decency not to pry into Navy affairs by inquiring as to the contents of the cartons. He presumably would not have been amused to learn that they contained dozens of my personal souvenirs, which I had acquired in a year of visiting ports of call in North Africa, Egypt, India, the Persian Gulf, and Australia.

Our "Long Voyage Home" was also memorable for a number of other reasons. In crossing the North Atlantic, our ship encountered the worst storm I had experienced in two years at sea. For several days and nights we were buffeted by gale-force winds and mountainous seas. In the daytime the mess halls were virtually empty, and at night we were in constant danger of being thrown from our bunks. I constantly thought of the possible irony of a shipload of Armed Service personnel surviving the war and then being lost en route home. Later that week, New York newspapers featured page-one photos of a Navy aircraft carrier which had ferried troops home from Europe, had encountered the same storm, and had the forward end of its flight deck bent upward to resemble a giant ski.

During the voyage I became acquainted with an Army Air Forces Dental Officer from the Midwest who had one of the most remarkable stories I heard during or after the war. Because of his age and marital status — married with children — he was clearly exempt from compulsory military service. Nev-

ertheless, he wanted to "do his part" and applied for an Army Air Forces
commission, assuring his family that he would never be sent overseas as all
dental work on servicemen would be done at stateside bases and stations.
Nevertheless, he was ordered out to an Army Air Forces base in India, from
which U.S. cargo planes were flying "over the hump" of the Himalayas to
supply our ally, Nationalist China. It was the doctor's responsibility to identify
victims of aircraft disasters from their dental records. What an assignment!

General Hase's arrival at a pier in the Hudson River on New Year's Eve, 31
December 1945, was also very memorable. On previous returns of Merchant
ships, the docks would usually be unoccupied except for a few longshoremen,
customs agents, and Navy Shore Patrol. But on this occasion the piers and
nearby buildings were draped with flags and bunting, a military band was
playing, and there were hundreds of relatives and friends awaiting the return
of their loved ones. It was an unforgettable experience for all of us.

Early in January, after completing another "Officer Going On Leave
Check-List" at the Armed Guard Center and securing the services of a Navy
truck to deliver my souvenirs to Railway Express, I was again en route to Fort
Wayne — this time after an absence of 16 months.

Chapter 17

1946 —
Decommissioning
the Armed Guard

In mid-January I returned to the Armed Guard Center in Brooklyn, expecting to wind up my Navy duty in a few days. I had more than enough "service points" to get out as soon as the paperwork could be processed. However, I was not really eager to return to civilian life as I was interested in "readjustment" as it was called, and I thought I might do a bit of job hunting in New York City.

To my surprise and gratification I was offered an interesting option. The Personnel Officer at the Center, WAVE Lieutenant Bea Ahlgren, USNR, told me that my record had been reviewed — a former enlisted man, Armed Guard Officer, survivor, etc. — and that I was considered qualified to become Aide to the new Commanding Officer, Captain William T. Swanston, USN, for the duration of the decommissioning of the Center. If I accepted, I would be recommended for promotion from Lieutenant to Lieutenant-Commander. Accepting the offer was an easy decision.

Captain Swanston, then nearing retirement, had been a U.S. Navy submarine officer during World War I and had served in World War II as the Commanding Officer of a Navy submarine tender in the Pacific. It was my first experience in reporting to a regular Annapolis-graduate Navy officer, and I found the experience to be very rewarding. Captain Swanston and I remained good friends for a number of years after the war.

In the large office which we shared, Captain Swanston was an interesting conversationalist and told me much about exploits of U.S. submarines in the Pacific, including the tragic story of USS *Tang*, under Commander Richard O'Kane, USN. Following a very successful patrol against Japanese shipping,

Above: The author with Captain William T. Swanston, USN, the last Commanding Officer of the Brooklyn Armed Guard Center, in January 1946. Below: The author credits WAVE Lieutenant "Bea" Ahlgren (r.), Personnel Officer at the AG Center, for the research and recommendation which resulted in his being promoted to Lieutenant Commander. (Photos, U.S. Navy)

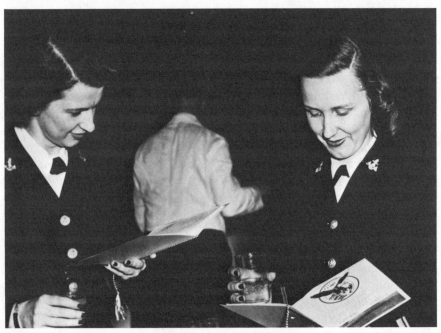

the *Tang* fired a last torpedo, which proved to have a faulty mechanism, causing it to arc through a wide circle underwater and return to sink the *Tang*.

I do not remember much about the administrative details of the decommissioning, although two rather amusing incidents stand out.

In his personal relationship with others, Captain Swanston was a warm and friendly officer and gentleman; however, he conducted his daily Captain's Mast with equal compassion or toughness depending upon the circumstances.

On one occasion, a Navy seaman, who had been AWOL and had turned himself in at the Center, made the mistake of bringing along his uncle, who was a defense attorney. Captain Swanston held that was unwarranted interference in the Navy's disciplinary system and put *both* of them in the brig!

The second incident involved the Officer's Wine Mess, which had been operating since early in the war and had accumulated a modest bank balance. Captain Swanston felt the profits should be contributed to Navy Relief. However, due to some technicality, that was not possible. As a result, the only solution was to dissipate all the profits by selling liquor at a loss for the final few weeks. The departing Armed Guard officers probably carried as many cases of spirits on New York subways as handled by any liquor distributor in town!

* * *

While helping to wind down the Center during duty hours, I spent my evenings and weekends back at the Henry Hudson Hotel in Manhattan, which was also winding down as a Navy BOQ. It became a kind of "Last Man's Club," where the usual topic of conversation was "What are you going to do now?"

During March or April, I was able to re-establish contact with Nelson Deranian of Indianapolis, who had been a close associate and friend at Great Lakes. Deranian had secured his release from the Office of Strategic Services (OSS) and had joined a law firm in Washington, D.C.

On one occasion he told me that he would be in New York City on business, and we made an appointment to have lunch at the Waldorf-Astoria — which led to several interesting experiences.

I recall that it was a rainy spring day as I rode the subway from Brooklyn to Manhattan, getting off at 51st Street and Lexington Avenue, only a short block north of the Waldorf. Trying to duck in and out of the rain, I entered the hotel through its ground-level garage, which extended through the building between 49th and 50th Streets near Lexington Avenue.

Suddenly I discovered that I was in a cavernous passageway, filled with a large number of uniformed New York City policemen.

One of them grabbed me and said, "Don't move. Just be quiet."

After a few moments, I asked, "What's going on here?"

I was told that Winston Churchill and his wife were on their way down from their suite to be picked up by limousine. I had read in the papers that Churchill, who had inexplicably been voted out as Prime Minister in the first postwar British election, was in New York to be honored by some organization like the English Speaking Union. His temporary political defeat may have been a blessing in disguise as it gave him time to write his great five-volume history of World War II.

Within a few minutes, Winnie and Clemmie came through the revolving door. Wearing his usual Homburg hat and smoking his usual cigar, he greeted the small group of onlookers with his famous "V for Victory" hand signal. From a distance of no more than 20 or 25 feet, I thought I noticed a sparkle in his eyes and recalled his well-known reputation for always having a cocktail or two before lunch and dinner.

* * *

Later, over lunch in the old Men's Bar of the Waldorf, Deranian and I had a memorable reunion. He told me of his tour of duty with OSS, during which he worked in the underground in Europe with Tito and his Partisans in Nazi-occupied Yugoslavia. I told him something of my experiences in the Moslem Middle East, from which Deranian's Armenian Christian parents had been refugees only one generation earlier.

In retrospect, I realize now, after four and one-half years in the U.S. Navy and considerable international travel, this unsophisticated Hoosier felt far more comfortable in New York's Waldorf-Astoria than he ever had at Fort Wayne's Keenan Hotel.

During my final month at the Armed Guard Center, Captain Swanston kindly gave me a few hours off from time to time in order that I could do some job hunting in Manhattan. I had previously contacted Nelson Rockefeller, who cooperated in setting up several interviews for me.

One of these was with an executive of Standard Oil, who offered me an opportunity to go to Venezuela "to learn the oil industry from the ground up." It was an interesting offer, but I had been away from home for too long to go abroad again. So I declined with thanks.

Still later I learned of what seemed to me a very exciting opportunity. Mr. Rockefeller set up an appointment for me with an executive of Rockefeller Center Corporation, who told me that plans were under discussion between the State of New York and New York City to create a kind of New York City Promotion and Trade Commission, which Mr. Rockefeller was to head. I was looked upon as a prospective advertising or public relations executive. It was not a lifetime career opportunity, but I felt it would afford me very interesting business and political contacts and experience. Unfortunately, the joint state-city financing never materialized.

Although my job-hunting efforts were not as fruitful as I had hoped, I had another more important bonus. I met in January and married in May a young Canadian gal, Helen Louise Sorley of Toronto, who had worked the Roosevelt-Churchill "hot line" for the Combined Chiefs of Staff in Washington, and who has now been my wife for over 44 years.

* * *

As I left the Armed Guard Center for the last time in mid-May, I recalled an old seaman's anecdote which I had heard a number of times during the war. To wit:

> When this damn war is over, I'm gonna put one of those oars from that lifeboat over my shoulder and start walking inland. When I reach a place where people begin asking, 'What's that you're carrying?' . . . that's where I'm gonna settle down!

I had served with the U.S. Navy for 52 months, 24 of them at sea. Had sailed about 250,000 miles, roughly 10 times around the world at the equator, which I crossed 12 times. Had visited at least 100 "faraway places" in the Caribbean, South America, Great Britain, Europe, Africa, the Middle East, Southeast Asia, and Australia.

Wanderlust? Enough was enough! Home Sweet Home!

But wait. There is a sequel to this story, which is like the contrived plot of a season-ending episode in a modern TV soap opera.

Helen and I were married at St. Patrick's Cathedral in New York in May 1946. Our first child, a daughter, was born in November 1947 while we were living in White Plains, New York. Because we had few friends and no relatives living in that area, we deferred the christening until the spring of 1948, when we went to Fort Wayne to visit my mother and brother and his family.

We made arrangements for the baptismal service at St. Patrick's Catholic Church, where I had been christened in 1914. I had not been to the church since my Fort Wayne-Chicago girlfriend and I had attended Midnight Mass there on Christmas Eve 1941.

When the appointment was made, we were told that there would be another christening at the same time, which was a common procedure for a Sunday afternoon.

Our little entourage consisted of my mother, my brother and his wife, two contemporary friends of mine — a young man and woman who were to serve as godfather and godmother — and, of course, my wife and I and our infant daughter.

Shortly after entering the baptismal room, we were joined by the other family for the christening of their first child. It was, believe it or not, my ex-girlfriend, her husband, their child, her father, and a local couple who were prewar friends of ours and were to serve as their witnesses.

We all nodded and smiled but exchanged no words. During the service, everyone in both parties was aware of the irony of the situation, except the girl's husband, my wife, and, of course, the two babies.

But that's not all. My brother eventually followed her father as president of a successor company, General Telephone of Indiana. Our daughter's godmother became a successful stockbroker and now lives in Palm Beach, Florida. Her godfather, then a local bank teller, is now a Bishop of the Catholic Church in Indiana. Our daughter, aged 42, happily married and mother of two children, is now an Episcopal Priest in the Diocese of Massachusetts. Our younger daughter, mother of three children, is married to a young magazine publisher, who is the son of a former U.S. Army officer and Australian woman who met in Melbourne during the war.

What a soap opera! Tune in again next season.

THE END

Stamford, Connecticut
May 1990

Epilogue

For the next 40 years, like most other veterans, I gave only occasional passing thought to World War II as I was busily occupied with earning a living, establishing a home, and raising a family.

However, in the early 1980s, after retiring from a large U.S. corporation, I decided, simply as a hobby, to do some historical research about the war, especially those aspects in which I had had some personal experiences, mainly certain events which occurred in Argentina and the South Atlantic in July 1944.

Through the good offices of the Naval Historical Center and the National Archives in Washington, D.C., I was able to tap a rich lode of information which, like all fields of study, continues to spread and grow to this very day.

To any veterans of any U.S. war or their descendants who happen to read this book, I strongly recommend similar research as a rewarding hobby. Since virtually all wartime documents have now been declassified and preserved in the National Archives, it is possible to locate military personnel lists, operating base histories, war diaries of various Army, Navy, and Coast Guard units, reports of training and combat activities, copies of military intelligence documents, etc. And it's easy to do — but easier in person than by correspondence.

As to the Merchant Marine, crew lists and other records were responsibilities of individual maritime lines, not the War Shipping Administration. Some operators maintained records after the war; others did not. Therefore, files are not available from public agencies.

When I visited the National Archives for the first time in 1980, I learned that that venerable establishment has a very modern operating system. First of all, there is a staff of research consultants who are available to advise new researchers by directing them to appropriate sections of the Archives. There are index card files which categorize and describe briefly each of the millions of documents in storage. There are research clerks who will locate and deliver to reading rooms the various files or documents desired. And, finally, there are duplicating services available which provide copies at nominal costs.

Like most other Americans, I had often criticized so-called "government bureaucracy," but I came to have great respect and admiration for the dedicated staff of the National Archives.

* * *

Following, capsulized by subject, are the results of my research into the circumstances of my experiences in World War II. Good luck to others who may undertake similar studies.

a. Fate of the Liberty Ships

Of the 2,710 Liberty ships built by American shipyards between 1941 and 1945, more than 200 were lost during the hostilities to enemy torpedoes and bombs and maritime accidents. The principal threat was German U-boats.

After the war the Liberties were considered too slow for competitive foreign shipping, but the world's commercial fleets had been decimated, and the United States was able to sell a major share of the surviving vessels to Allied governments.

The remaining Liberties were "moth-balled" in American ports and rivers. During the following decades, most were sold for scrap. By the 1980s only two were still in existence in this country — SS *Jeremiah O'Brien*, now a maritime museum in San Francisco, and SS *John W. Brown*, soon to play a similar role in Baltimore. The author visited both ships while researching this book.

As to my own Liberty ships, I knew that *William Gaston* was lying on the bottom of the South Atlantic, but I wondered what had happened to the *Alfred Moore*. I was pleased to learn that she had survived the war and had continued in commercial service until 1961, when she was scrapped in Bremerhaven, Germany.

b. Fate of the U-boats

Before and during the war, Nazi Germany built and launched a total of 1,162 *Unterseeboots* starting with the small 250-ton Type IIs, which became known as "canoes," continuing through the 750-ton Type VIIs, which primarily fought the Battle of the Atlantic, to the 1,600-ton Type IXs, which were used for long-range operations and for service as supply ships, known as "milch cows." As the war progressed, the smaller types which survived were used to train new crews in the Baltic Sea.

Between 3 September 1939 and 8 May 1945, a total of 785 U-boats were destroyed, principally by British and American Naval and Air Forces. On Victory-In-Europe Day, all U-boat commanders still at sea were ordered by Admiral Doenitz, then Hitler's successor as Fuhrer, to proceed to Allied seaports and surrender. Approximately 150 did so at ports all the way from Narvik, Norway, to Portsmouth, New Hampshire. These were later scuttled in the North Atlantic by the Allied Navies in what was known as "Operation Deadlight." Another 150 boats were scuttled by their own crews in defiance of orders. Two others, including *U-977* under command of Kapitan-Leutnant Hans Schaeffer, sailed all the way to the Rio del la Plata to surrender to "friendly" Argentina.

During the war the U-boats were crewed by a total of some 39,000 men, of whom 32,000 were lost at sea — the highest fatality rate for any major force in the entire history of warfare. Ironically, the Allied Merchant Fleets lost approximately the same number of men during the same period.

c. The Adversary of SS *William Gaston*

The never-seen enemy who torpedoed and sank *William Gaston* in July 1944 in the South Atlantic was Kriegsmarine Commander Jurgen Oesten, Captain of German *U-boat 861*. I not only learned this from German documents now available in Washington, but I also was able to contact Commander Oesten, who survived the war and now lives in Hamburg, Germany.

During the past eight years, Commander Oesten and I have carried on an intermittent correspondence. In 1983, while on a trip to Europe, my wife and I were guests of Jurgen and Edith Oesten at their home in Hamburg. In 1986, they visited our home in Stamford, Connecticut.

Commander Oesten is a remarkable man for whom I have developed great respect and admiration. He was born in Berlin, in October 1913, into what was hardly a militaristic household. His father was an accomplished sculptor. In 1931, he secured an appointment to the German Naval Academy at Flensburg. Upon graduation, he volunteered for the U-boat service and when war broke out in September 1939, he was already in command of *U-61* at age 25.

He later commanded *U-106* and, after three successful years at sea attacking Allied shipping, he was given several shore duties as a U-boat Flotilla Commander and later on the staff of Admiral Karl Doenitz, Chief of U-boats. In the latter assignment, he met Adolph Hitler for the first time and has described the Fuhrer as "mad but mesmerizing."

In late 1943, he was given his third command, *U-861*, which he took on a year-long patrol to the east coast of South America, the Cape of Good Hope,

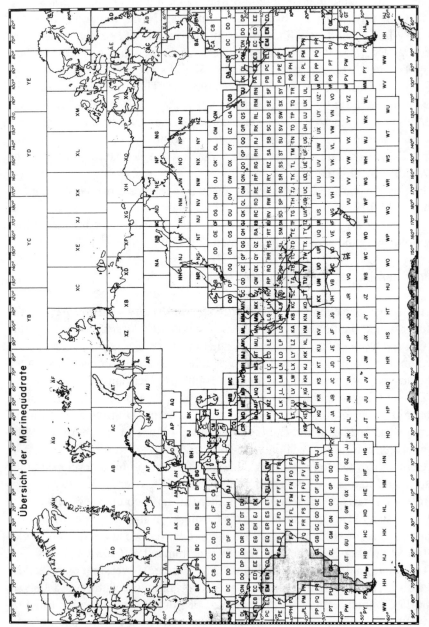

The western portion of the German Navy worldwide alpha-numerical navigation grid system, established to reduce errors in radio transmissions of positions by degrees and minutes of latitude and longitude. (Kriegsmarine document)

the Indian Ocean, and Malaysia, where *U-861* was one of a number of cargo-carrying U-boats which delivered technical manufactured goods to the Japanese and picked up critical raw materials for return to Germany. In addition to its role as an underwater freighter, *U-861* also successfully attacked five Allied cargo ships and tankers, including *William Gaston*.

In January 1945, U-boat headquarters ordered all of its boats in the Indian Ocean to return to their bases. Between mid-January and mid-April, *U-861* successfully made the 10,000-mile transit from Malaysia to North Atlantic waters, finally arriving on 19 April at Trondheim, Norway, because all continental U-boat bases had been lost to the Allies.

Following the end of hostilities in Europe, Oesten told me, he was ordered to sail *U-861* from Norway to Liverpool, England, where the critical raw materials from Malaysia were off-loaded. Later, Oesten's boat was one of about 100 U-boats scuttled by the Allies in the North Atlantic — in order, he believes, to preclude any question of sharing them with the Russians.

After the war, in cooperation with several Danish businessmen who had refrigeration patents and manufacturing facilities, Oesten founded two German firms in Hamburg which designed and installed air conditioning systems aboard ships. His businesses prospered, spreading to other seaports in Europe, the Middle East, and Far East. In 1985, he sold his holdings and retired to live comfortably in residential Hamburg, where he continues his hobbies — traveling, photography, and yachting.

Among his close friends in Hamburg are several other former U-boat captains, including Commander Peter "Ali" Cremer, whose book *U-boat Commander*, describing his experiences on *U-333* between 1942 and 1943, was published in 1984 by Naval Institute Press.

When Oesten and his wife visited the McCormicks in 1986, he was on his *fifth* trip around the world — one as a midshipman, three as an international businessman, and one as a vacationing retiree. Seeming never to stop achieving, at age 76, he now types long letters in several languages on his personal computer!

Jurgen Oesten is, in my judgment, a kind of latter-day Renaissance man.

d. Nazi Spies in Argentina

From a declassified 1946 FBI document, "German Espionage in Latin America," I obtained a very comprehensive report of Nazi activity in Argentina. This had been widely suspected during the war, but the FBI records were very specific.

The Nazi government actually had two espionage agencies operating in Argentina: ABWEHR, the intelligence branch of the Wehrmacht (German Armed Forces), which functioned through the German Embassy, and

Four former U-boat captains in Hamburg on the occasion of the publication of *U-Boat Commander* by Peter "Ali" Cremer. L. to r.: Claus Korth, Cremer, Jurgen Oesten, and Otto Kretschmer. The book was later published in English by the U.S. Naval Institute Press. (Photo, courtesy of Jurgen Oesten)

Sicherheitsdienst, known as SD, which was the espionage arm of the Nazi Party and operated in the underground.

SD was staffed by agents who had been sent to Argentina as representatives of German firms. The leader of the group was Johannes Siegfried Becker, known as the "Hauptsturmführer," who was born in Leipzig in 1912, became a Second Lieutenant of Infantry in the German Army, and in 1937 was sent by the Nazis to Buenos Aires as a representative of Deutsche Handwerks Gesellschaft of Berlin.

From 1943 to 1944, SD operated at least nine clandestine shortwave radio stations in and around Buenos Aires, sending nightly dispatches to Germany regarding Allied ship movements, and other economic, political, and military reports.

"Hauptsturmführer" Becker was supported in his espionage efforts by a colorful cast of German, Argentine, and Spanish agents, including Wilhelm Seidlitz, Argentine representative for German National Railways; Gustav Utzinger, Argentine manager for the German electronics firm, Telefunken; and Ulrich Daue, former Chief Radio Operator on the German freighter *Tacoma*, which had been the supply ship to *Graf Spee*, and many others.

Opposite: German *U-boat 861* and her crew before sailing from Kiel in April 1944. Commander Oesten (inset) is in the front row, first white sword belt from the left. (Photo, courtesy of Foto-Druppel, Wilhelmshaven)

Throughout the war, SD in Argentina was financed by the Hitler government in Berlin and the German business community in Buenos Aires and enjoyed the toleration, if not active support, of the Argentine government.

SD was successful in organizing the escape of 232 *Graf Spee* internees, most of whom returned to Europe aboard "neutral" Spanish ships. However, SD reports of Allied ship movements were less productive.

In his memoirs, *Ten Years and Twenty Days*, Admiral Doenitz reported that throughout the war German agents in Latin America had reported the departures of Allied Naval and Merchant vessels but that those reports were rarely productive because of the difficulty for lone U-boats in the South Atlantic to operate against convoys or to locate independent ships on the vast sea.

In 1944, a plan to operate an Argentine spy ship to pursue Allied vessels and report their positions at sea must have seemed like a very good idea.

e. The Argentine Spy Ship

On 9 July 1944, while *William Gaston* was discharging cargo in Montevideo, Lieutenant-Commander Carl W. Finstrom, USNR, (referred to in Chapter 9) Naval Intelligence Officer at the U.S. Embassy in Buenos Aires, wrote a classified report to the Office of Naval Intelligence in Washington, which was approved and forwarded by Captain W. W. Webb, USN. It reported that "a new shipping concern has appeared on the scene" and that "one vessel, *Besugo*, has a *radio-telephone* on board." ("Intelligence Report," serial: 419-44).

This report, found at the National Archives in 1982, was the first documentation I was able to locate regarding the possible identity of the small Argentine vessel which followed *William Gaston* out of Buenos Aires on 19 July 1944. The existence then of a radio-telephone on an old, small Argentine freighter was very surprising and suspicious. However, its reported ownership by the Bembergs, a wealthy Argentine Jewish family, presumably anti-Nazi in political persuasion, seemed to give the operation a purely commercial and legitimate status.

f. Research in Argentine

Although U.S. Naval and FBI intelligence reports about Nazi espionage in Argentina were very comprehensive, I felt the need for on-the-spot research in Buenos Aires.

Through the good offices of the English-language *Buenos Aires Herald*, I was able to establish contact and a working relationship with an Argentine journalist-historian, Baroness Lida von Schey-Korolma, who holds dual

Argentine-British citizenship, who had worked for the British Embassy during World War II, had been South American coordinator for the BBC following the war, and, upon retirement from the post, had been honored with a Member, Order of the British Empire (MBE) by Queen Elizabeth II. Lida's ancestors were ancient Irish with the family name of McGillicuddy!

By extraordinary coincidences, Baroness von Schey had unique personal experiences with the events under study. While living in Uruguay in December 1939, she and her family had witnessed the scuttling of *Graf Spee* off Montevideo. Also, she was personally acquainted with the Bembergs and was immediately convinced that they would have had no involvement with a pro-Nazi spy ship. Finally, she and her Austrian-English husband had been close personal friends of USN Lieutenant-Commander Finstrom, author of the "*Besugo* Report," who had been godfather to their first child.

Although wartime documents in Argentina are not as readily available to the public as in the United States, Baroness von Schey was able to fill in several "missing links" in the story. Among other things, she was able to establish that the Bembergs had no connection whatever with the Argentine spy ship, that the vessel had in fact been owned and operated by Dolphin Shipping Company, one of several Argentine steamship lines which had been "black listed" by the Allies early in the war for "pro-Axis activities." The 1944 Buenos Aires Telephone Directory revealed that Dolphin and Cosadex, owner of *Besugo* had the same street address and telephone number. Baroness von Schey also obtained a 1944 photo of *Besugo* taken in the Rio de la Plata.

g. The *Graf Spee* Prisoners

After Argentina, reluctantly and under Allied pressure, declared war on the Axis powers in March 1945, the *Graf Spee* internees became prisoners of war. They were transferred to restricted compounds in and around Buenos Aires, and the enlisted men in particular were denied further freedom of movement.

Of *Graf Spee's* original complement of 1,055 surviving officers and men (including the 19 civilians aboard), 232 had escaped back to Germany, 285 had married (mostly to Argentine women), and seven had died. A total of 816, including those who had married, were regarded as German prisoners of war in Argentina on V-E Day, 8 May 1945.

For the first nine months after the war — actually, for five months after V-J Day — the *Graf Spee* prisoners were in a kind of limbo, with a low priority on the list of the world's postwar problems. They were not "men without a country," but men without available transportation to their homeland.

Early in 1946, the British agreed to repatriate the *Graf Spee* prisoners back to Germany. For that purpose, they ordered one of their troopships, HMS *Highland Monarch*, to Buenos Aires and Montevideo to pick up the Germans.

And, in an almost classic example of English poesy, the British *also* dispatched, to serve as an escort, the light cruiser HMS *Ajax*, which had been one of *Graf Spee's* adversaries in the Battle of the River Plate in December 1939. Three of *Ajax's* 1939 crew were still aboard.

The two British ships arrived in Buenos Aires on 11 February. On 15 February, 811 prisoners were taken on board plus an unknown number of "other German undesirables." On 16 February, an additional 75 prisoners, including internees from the German supply ship *Tacoma*, were brought aboard by launch from Montevideo. The two British ships then departed for Hamburg, Germany.

According to a U.S. Naval Intelligence Report of 23 February 1946, 37 Argentine wives of German seamen signified their intention to sail with their husbands, but only six actually boarded the *Highland Monarch*.

As the two British ships sailed down the Rio de la Plata toward the open sea, they passed close abeam the wreckage of *Graf Spee*. All of the Germans crowded to the starboard rail for one last look at their old ship. Some saluted with pride, some stood in silence, and some cried.

As a footnote to history, it should be recorded that, of the nearly 900 Germans who sailed on the *Highland Monarch*, more than 400 eventually returned to Argentina to settle permanently. Among the *Graf Spee* officers who had escaped to Germany in the early 1940s, Lieutenant-Commander Friedrich Wilhelm Razenack also returned to Argentina, married an Argentine woman, and eventually joined the large German colony which has settled in Cordoba Province. There is now a popular Oktoberfest — held in April in the Southern Hemisphere!

In 1979, my Argentine friend, Baroness von Schey, became acquainted with Commander Razenack when she worked on a television documentary for the BBC, commemorating the 40th anniversary of the Battle of the River Plate, which included still-living crew members from British, German, and New Zealand ships. Commander Razenack was the spokesman for German survivors. Baroness von Schey served as consultant to the BBC, as she had done for several decades after the war.

h. Cafe Ta-Ba-Ris

Ta-Ba-Ris no longer exists in Buenos Aires, although it is remembered well by its wartime patrons, mostly local Lotharios, naval and maritime officers from visiting ships, and even foreign newspaper correspondents. Some men recall that most of its hostesses were attractive Hungarian women.

Because in mid-July 1944, *Besugo* was apparently moored in Rio de la Plata near *William Gaston*, and her officers were believed to be observing the activities of the Americans, it seems likely that the officers of both ships were at Ta-Ba-Ris on the evening of Wednesday, 18 July, when the whole house was bidding goodbye to the departing American ship.

And because Ta-Ba-Ris was a demimonde kind of establishment, it seems possible that the owner-manager and some of the staff may have been aware of the secret mission of *Besugo*. Even the lovely Argentine vocalist Maria may have known. What other explanation was there for her strange interest in the wives and children of *William Gaston* crew members?

i. The Mysterious Sailing Ship

While the story of Ta-Ba-Ris and *Besugo* are still subject to some speculation, details of other events of July 1944 are now well known. For example, according to FBI documents, on 22 July 1944, a sailing ship named *Santa Barbara*, formerly the German *Passim*, but then flying the Portuguese flag, arrived off the Argentine coast near Mar del Plata. Her Master was Hein Garber, a German yachtsman.

With the aid of rubber boats, *Santa Barbara* landed two new pro-German agents plus a quantity of Argentine pesos and a shipment of German chemicals, which could be converted into additional pesos. For her return trip, the vessel picked up two other German spies whose identities had become known to the Provincial Police of Buenos Aires.

There now seems no doubt whatever that *Santa Barbara* was the sailing vessel which had passed southbound abeam of *William Gaston* on the evening of 21 July 1944.

j. The Fate of SS *Matagorda*

There is also no doubt whatever as to the ultimate fate of the U.S. Navy seaplane tender.

Following rescue of the *William Gaston* crew in July 1944, USS *Matagorda* and the Mariners from PBM Squadron #203 continued their anti-submarine patrols of the western South Atlantic, operating from various bases up and down the coast of Brazil. Quoting from the ship's official war diary:

On 29 August 1944, while operating out of Fortaleza, *Matagorda* rescued five survivors of a downed PBY5 plus the crew from an assisting PBM.

Matagorda made numerous runs along the coast during supply and training missions. Based at Recife, she visited many Brazilian ports, including Victoria, Natal, the island of Fernando de Noronha, Bahia, and Rio de Janeiro. She departed Recife 1 April 1945, touched briefly at San Juan, and reached Norfolk 14 April. From 2 June to 6 July, she made two runs to Bermuda and Puerto Rico, returning to Norfolk with men of seaplane squadrons.

Matagorda steamed to New York 10 July to begin conversion to a press information ship. As such, her mission would be to provide all proper news facilities for the Allied press and transport them to the coast of Japan, where they would cover the projected operations "Olympic" and "Coronet," the invasion of Japan. Reclassified as AG-122 on 30 July, her conversion was halted in early September when Japan surrendered.

Following V-J Day, USS *Matagorda* was decommissioned in February 1946, at which time Commander Crinkley retired, and the USNR crews of *Matagorda* and PBM Squadron #203 were either transferred to other ships or were honorably discharged and/or placed on inactive duty.

In 1949, *Matagorda* was transferred to the U.S. Coast Guard and commissioned as a weather ship in the Pacific Ocean. In 1969, again decommissioned, she was sunk off Hawaii in a U.S. Navy bomber training exercise.

Thus, of the four ships which "passed in the night" off Brazil in July 1944, USS *Matagorda* joined SS *William Gaston* and German *U-861* at the bottom of the sea, thousands of miles apart. *Besugo* was scrapped in the 1950s.

k. *Besugo*'s Mission: Success or Failure?

Based on *Besugo*'s now known antecedents and her strange behavior in July 1944, there has never been any doubt in my mind that it was the mission of the small Argentine ship to pursue *William Gaston* into the South Atlantic and daily to report her position, course, and speed for the purpose of setting up the American ship for attack by a German U-boat.

In fact, for over 40 years, the only subsidiary question in my mind was whether *Besugo* had communicated directly with *U-861* by means of her radio-telephone, or whether she had made her reports to U-boat headquarters in Germany for relay to U-boats at sea in the South Atlantic.

In my previous correspondence and meetings with Commander Oesten, I had not pressed him on details of the war because I found that he was not much interested in discussing them. Because the war was even more tragic for Germany than for the Allies, Oesten seemed disinclined to relive it. I respected his privacy.

Nevertheless, in a letter written early in 1988, I decided to press Oesten for a specific answer. Did he communicate directly with *Besugo* or did he receive his information by relay from U-boat headquarters?

To my surprise or amazement, Oesten told me that he had received no position reports from either source. And, because I regard him as a friend and honorable man, I accept his word.

He told me that at dusk on Sunday, 23 July, while *U-861* was on a southeasterly course en route to the Cape of Good Hope, one of his lookouts on the bridge reported a Liberty ship in the distance. For two hours Oesten maintained visual and hydrophone contact with *William Gaston* and, after dark and on the surface, he was able by superior speed, despite mountainous seas, to achieve a position on the starboard, weather side of the Liberty ship, in order, as he described it, "to assure a smooth run of the torpedoes."

I still feel that *Besugo* was trying to set us up, but fate apparently intervened.

On 22 July, Com Fourth Fleet had ordered *William Gaston* to change course to eastward to avoid coastal waters, where *U-861* had sunk a Brazilian auxiliary troopship on 20 July with a loss of 101 lives. It was a logical military decision under the circumstances. However, if *William Gaston* had continued her coastal course to Rio de Janeiro, she undoubtedly would have escaped *U-861*.

Alas, the fortunes of war!

Bibliography

Bekker, Cajus, *Hitler's Naval War*. New York: Doubleday and Company, 1974.

Busch, Harold. *U-Boats at War*. Bielefeld, Germany: Deutsche Heimat Verlag, 1954.

Cremer, Peter. *U-Boat Commander*. Annapolis: U.S. Naval Institute Press, 1984.

Diplomats and Demagogues, Memoirs of U.S. Ambassador to Argentina Spruille Braden. New York: Arlington House, 1950.

Frank, Wolfgang. *Die Wolf und der Admiral*. Hamburg: Kohler Verlag, 1953.

Garlinski, Joseph. *The Enigma War*. New York: Charles Scribner's Sons, 1980.

Gasaway, E.B. *Grey Wolf, Grey Sea*. New York: Ballantine Books, 1970.

German Espionage in Argentina, declassified FBI monograph. Washington, D.C.: U.S. Government Printing Office, 1946.

Hoyt, Edwin P. *The Death of the U-boats*. New York: McGraw-Hill Book Co., 1988.

Hughes, Terry, and John Costello. *The Battle of the Atlantic*. New York: The Dial Press/James Wade, 1977.

Josephs, Ray. *Argentine Diary*. New York: Random House, 1944.

Kahn, David. *Hitler's Spies*. New York: MacMillan Publishing Company, Inc., 1978.

Lenton, H.T. *Navies of the Second World War*, Vol. 2, *Submarine*. London: McDonald, 1965.

Middlebrook, Martin, *Convoy*. London: Allen Lane, 1976.

Noli, Jean. *The Admiral's Wolfpack*. New York: Doubleday and Company, 1974.

Rohwer, Jurgen. *Die U-Boot-Erfolge der Achsenmachte, 1939-1945*. Munich: J. F. Lehmanns Verlag, 1965.

Ruge, Friedrich. *Der Seekrieg (The Sea War)*. Stuttgart: Koehlers Verlag, 1954.

Russell, Francis. *The Secret War*. New York: Time-Life Books, 1981.

Schaeffer, Lieutenant-Commander Heinz. *U-977*. Hamburg: Kohler Verlag, 1956.

Shellenberg, Walter. *Hitler's Secret Service*. New York: Harper & Row, 1956.

Showell, J.P. Mallmann. *U-Boats Under the Swastika*. New York: Arco Publishing Company, 1973.

Ten Years and Twenty Days, The Memoirs of Grand Admiral Karl Doenitz. London: Weidenfeld and Nicolson, 1959.

Von der Porlen, Edward P. *The German Navy in World War II*. New York: Thomas Y. Crowell Company, 1968.

Werner, Herbert A. *Iron Coffins*. London: Arthur Barker, 1970.

World War II, Encyclopedia. Chicago: Rand McNally, 1977.

Index

Compiled by Lori L. Daniel

Other titles available from

Sunflower University Press ®

CAMPAIGN RIBBONS, by John R. Simmons.

PASSAGES TO FREEDOM: A Story of Capture and Escape, by Joseph S. Frelinghuysen.

SOME EARLY BIRDS, by Joe Hill.

AMERICAN FARM TOOLS: From Hand-Power to Steam-Power, by R. Douglas Hurt.

INSIDER AT SAC: Operations Analysis Under General LeMay, by Carroll L. Zimmerman.

KANSAS BOOTLEGGERS, by Patrick G. O'Brien and Kenneth J. Peak.

Complete backlist upon request.

Sunflower University Press ®
1531 Yuma (Box 1009)
Manhattan, Kansas 66502-4228
Phone 913-539-1888